MW01492103

Laurence Dougier

MEDITERRANEAN LIVING

PHOTOGRAPHY
Nicolas Mathéus

VENDOME
NEW YORK · LONDON

A PLACE IN THE SUN

Our senses take us back to our memories. We can still feel the sun in our eyes, the relentless heady heat, our ears filled with the familiar song of the cicadas. Fleeting memories of summer float by; leisurely meals that never seem to end, naps under olive trees, and the feeling of diving into the shimmering sea.

Mallorca, Menorca, Uzès, Skopelos, Comporta—the landscapes, raw beauty, and sunshine of the south have always called to me. This sense of freedom that I enjoyed throughout the sun-scorched trails of my youth owes a lot to a south where the sky explodes with an intense but nameless blue. When I began my career as a journalist-stylist, I knew I needed to travel to these Mediterranean places to find the purest *fincas*, old farms, fishing huts, ruined fortresses, and authentic farmhouses; all renovated, enthusiastically restored by owners, architects and designers adept at working with these almost mythical places. They skillfully blend vernacular architecture with radical new perspectives to achieve a sense of the essential, seen through the lens of resurrection and of breathing life into something anew. My own research has been rooted in these kinds of connections, these rich dialogues between the past and the present, brought to life in remarkable homes.

On this project, photographer Nicolas Mathéus and I traveled through Italy, Croatia, the Balearics, Provence, Portugal, and Greece to immortalize these unique and wonderful houses. Each one opened up to reveal its secrets, its inner life, its unexpected story. And now they are here for you to enjoy as you turn the pages.

Head south to a place in the sun.

—LAURENCE DOUGIER

MAJESTIC PEACE

LOPUD, CROATIA

PREVIOUS SPREAD
The superb 3.5 × 10 m pool and poolside overlook the Adriatic Sea and the Elaphiti Islands. It was built using stones from the Diocletian palace in Split. The pool is embedded in the ruins of an old village. Designed by David Kelly from RRP, the garden extends over the hill, planted with olive and cypress trees, santolina, and rosemary. It's a wonderful maze to lose yourself in. The chaise longues were sourced in the United States.

OPPOSITE
Large tables sit in the shade of a vine-covered arbor. The table was created from an industrial workbench and is covered by a cotton tablecloth and lined with vintage chairs by Tolix. The garden has a stunning sea view. The beautiful garden view runs all the way to the sea. The landscape gardener had to tame the wild brush and stony ground to create the beautiful green ensemble of Mediterranean plants.

The ferry you take from Dubrovnik is straight out of an antique etching. And the journey is a memory you'll keep coming back to—the boat's wake on the clear waters of the Adriatic, the string of wild islands, and then arriving on the island of Lopud next to the five-hundred-year-old Franciscan monastery, Notre-Dame de la Grotte. Behind the port, the landscape is full of cypress and olive trees, and vine terraces. New Yorkers, interior designer Lucien Rees Roberts and architect Steven Harris fell head over heels for this sweeping view devoid of cars. "Lopud is a bit of a secret island," Lucien explains. "We discovered it through architect Antonio Zaninovic, who came across it by chance when he was tracing his grandfather's roots." This protected place proved irresistible. "You don't expect to encounter an almost untouched environment like this in the middle of Europe," the interior architect enthuses. "Then it took us four years to find and restore this fifteenth-century building set high up on the island. The Republic of Venice once reached as far as here; originally there was a defensive citadel and bunkers."

Antonio took care of the restoration. Although he is best known for his contemporary work, he chose to accentuate the beauty of the old stone, adding refined details with care so as to avoid ruining the authenticity of the building. For the rooms, Steven and Lucien—through their respective agencies in New York, Steven Harris Architects and RRP (previously Rees Roberts + Partners)—opted for an exquisite style; contemporary furniture was quickly put in place to create a dialogue with artworks collected from here and there.

The terraced garden enjoys sweeping views over the lush landscape of the Elaphiti Islands. The swimming pool was created using stone from a ruined palace in Split and sits perfectly in the Mediterranean garden, with direct access to the sea. The stubborn brush, sterile earth, and rocks had to be cleared before carobs, olive, and cypress trees could cover this idyllic refuge in a symphony of color.

RIGHT
The majestic primary bedroom features a mix of neutral limewashed walls, and a floor laid with slabs of local stone. 1960s wooden bedside lamp with concrete base, United States. 1960s wooden armchair with suede seat and back. *Fleeting Moment #1* (2014) by South African John Murray hangs on the wall.

A section of the living room faces the garden, also enjoying views of the ocean as far as the eye can see. A 1947 Charlotte Perriand straw chair and a Christian Liaigre oak stool next to two sofas designed by RRP. A Dogon sculpture from the end of the nineteenth century sits on a plinth.

BELOW

The long concrete shelves and bleached oak storage units in the kitchen designed by architect Antonio Zaninovic were made in situ. The central island is made entirely of béton brut with an integrated hob. Set of earthenware vases. The bespoke table was made by Beau Studio, Atlanta, and is lit from above by a 1950s paper light by American-Japanese designer Isamu Noguchi. Around the table, chairs from the same era by designer duo Audoux-Minet.

OPPOSITE

The exposed walls and local stone slabs of the kitchen create an understated, functional ambiance. The furniture and artworks are finds from the owners' travels, chosen with care and brought back from the US, Africa, and elsewhere. The result is a series of pleasant contrasts between different styles and eras.

FOLLOWING SPREAD

The huge living space is a bold blend of different styles—original or made to measure by European artisans. In the foreground, Paillé wood and straw armchair by Charlotte Perriand, from around 1935, and a 1940s lamp in an American design. RRP agency designed the sofa; the coffee table has a travertine top and a metal base; 1950s velour armchair; Spanish handmade rug, José Manuel Molina. Next to the sofa, Earth Goddess ceramic lamp, Atelier Démiurge Éditions. In the background to the left, Bodil Kjær desk and a 1960s French lacquered bronze sculpture bought at Christie's New York.

10

PREVIOUS SPREAD
David Kelly made the magnificent garden looking over the Adriatic into a paradise planted with a mix of Mediterranean plants. It is full of vigorous rosemary, boxwood, olive trees, cypress, and a host of flowering plants. A comfortable built-in stone bench scattered with seat pads and green and patterned linen cushions from Maison de Vacances. Sol y Luna aluminum chairs by Brown Jordan, 1954, and 1950s side tables by Eero Saarinen.

ABOVE
Built on the ruins of fifteenth-century defensive bunkers, the home renovated by architect Antonio Zaninovic looks as though it has been there forever. Its exterior walls are adorned with climbing plants and its pergola topped by a vigorous vine; the outside room and terraces invite you to enjoy unendingly lazy days.

OPPOSITE
The bathroom is functional with a pared-back feel. It features neutral limewashed walls with wooden storage and a polished concrete counter. The floor is laid with stone slabs that continue into the shower. Faucets, Vola, and linen towels, Lissoy.

16

MOUNTAINS AND MARVELS

DEIÀ, MALLORCA, SPAIN

PREVIOUS SPREAD
The infinity pool enjoys breath-taking views over the landscape, with reflections of Deià. Mountains and olive fields surround the garden terraces that have small private spaces, allowing you to make the most of the spectacular setting.

OPPOSITE
The terrace is set for an early evening drink. Iron and glass double doors made by ironmonger Toni Calafell open from the kitchen onto a lush garden. Two superb palm trees fringe an arrangement of simple, low wicker stools and a coffee table.

London-based creative fashion director Yasmin Yusuf loves places with soul, beautiful views, and hills. The village of Deià on the northern coast of Mallorca was the natural choice for her to build her holiday home.

Here, she was able to make her dreams of open spaces, organic curves and an abundance of light come true with the help of renowned architects Oro Del Negro and Manuel Villanueva, founders of Moredesign agency. "The house softens angles in both form and spirit," she says. "As soon as I discovered the work of these two young architects, I knew I wanted them to lead on my summer home that sits between the sea and the mountains."

Embracing her mischievous nature and love of the eclectic, Yasmin imagined the building in her own image—a glorious mix of styles with hippie chic accents. Built over three floors with an abundance of curves and large metal-framed windows looking out onto nature—the location radiates a holiday ambience. "We integrated the house into its natural setting as subtly as we could, often by using reclaimed materials. We wanted to create a natural flow between the outside and the inside, opening it up as much as possible so the owners could experience an inside-out lifestyle," explain Oro and Manuel. "We had the help of the amazing builder Jaime Salas, who knows better than anyone how to make our plans and ideas a reality, as well as overcome any obstacles."

The lush garden is terraced with endless Mediterranean views. Next to the infinity pool with its huge daybeds made for lazy days, the view over the village of Deià is sublime, accented by hundred-year-old olive trees all the way to the blue of the sea.

RIGHT
Set on a hillside, the dry-stone walls of the house and the vine-covered, reed shades of its terraces help it blend with the natural landscape.

ABOVE
The gently organic shapes of the
kitchen blend elegant and rustic
styling; the ultra-functional
kitchen designed by Moredesign
was made in *tadelakt*—a traditional Moroccan lime-based plaster
finish—with bespoke whitewashed
wood storage units. Yasmin is
fond of crockery and displays her
special finds on the brick shelving.

OPPOSITE
The dining room is adjacent to
the kitchen and has a steel-edged
pine table and benches, as well
as a custom brickwork bench.
Yasmin's glassware collection is
displayed here with its tones of
amber and ochre. Vases, stemmed
glasses, carafes—found at Gordiola
in Palma, and the flea markets of
Mallorca, Lille, Paris, London, Pasa-
dena and New York—are displayed
on the shelves set into the wall.

PREVIOUS SPREAD
The swimming pool is located below the house, sheltered from the wind in a special spot looking out over the surrounding mountains and the village. Large daybeds crafted from reclaimed wood by Pedro Casanovas rest on the smooth concrete poolside area—an invitation to spend lazy days in the shade of the trees.

ABOVE
The house is arranged over three floors with a beautiful central stairway made by Oro Del Negro and Manuel Villanueva. The simple steps are polished concrete, the banister and guardrails sleek steel—creating a barely there appeal. As ever with these two architects, embellishments are stripped away.

OPPOSITE
Yasmin's vaulted, high-ceilinged bedroom sits on the second floor and is split into three distinct areas. Partition walls form the bedroom with touches of lilac and ochre, the bathroom with its vintage copper tub and rough stone washbasin, and a large dressing room with a huge wardrobe.

26

A HAVEN ON HIGH

MENORCA, SPAIN

PREVIOUS SPREAD
Set on a hillside overlooking sixty hectares of wild landscape, the whole of the nineteenth century *finca* is whitewashed. Its pristine outline appears at the end of an idyllic country lane lined with the low stone walls so characteristic of the Balearic Islands.

OPPOSITE
The blend of materials and colors in the vast vaulted hallway successfully pull the décor together. A Nanimarquina rug picks out the colors in the work *Eagle's Break 2018*, commissioned from the artist Ezra Siegel, and the cement tiles whose colors were reworked by Atelier du Pont in Paris. Cane Nomad chairs from Norr11; natural wood bench and stool made by Carpintería Gavila in Mahón. Bird floor lamp in the background, Roche Bobois.

RIGHT
The architects designed a made-to-measure long stone table for the outside dining room. Bolonia chairs from iSiMAR match the walls. A handsome white stairway at the side takes you up to another terrace. This huge bedroom on the second floor is in camaïeu blue. The headboard designed by Atelier du Pont echoes the vintage armchair and footstool, found at El Recibidor in Barcelona, and the Nanimarquina rug.

FOLLOWING SPREAD
Above a view of endless olive trees, the outside space is made for relaxing. The twenty-five-meter swimming pool is laid with green pâte de verre mosaic tiles with a poolside area in local stone. After a dip you can head to the pool house and its kitchen and enjoy a meal by the water's edge.

Perched looking out over a sixty-hectare estate of remote Menorcan landscape, this magnificent nineteenth-century *finca* wears its new look well—skillfully undertaken by Paris architecture studio Atelier du Pont. The impressive building is surrounded by gardens and low stone walls that merge with the surrounding hillside. Its name is both fierce and elegant—Es Bec d'Aguila or "The Eagle's Beak." And it has certainly taken flight when it comes to luxury and refinement.

"The *finca* was left abandoned for many years. Everything had to be done from scratch," recalls its Menorcan owner, Benedicta Linares Pearce. The plans by architect Anne-Cécile Comar and her team, alongside local firm ARU Arquitectura, saw the building's one thousand square meters split over three floors. "We wanted to make the most of the amazing 360-degree panorama so that the twelve bedrooms and living rooms could enjoy unparalleled views of this beautiful island," is how she describes the huge rebuild she led from beneath the building's well-worn vaults.

The use of local materials and expertise—like wonderful *hidráulicos* cement tiles that are traditional on the island, and powder pink and verdigris built-in furniture—are evocative of the farms of long ago. Vintage furniture is from Spain, England, France, and Denmark—an eclectic approach that echoes Menorca's own history and its characteristically European identity. Es Bec d'Aguila mirrors the life of its owner: "I spent many years abroad with my husband, Benoît," Benedicta explains. "After having our three children, we finally decided to buy a house on the island where I was born and create a beautiful Iberian refuge."

The family can play happily in the long twenty-five-meter swimming pool set in the middle of a fabulous environment. The estate is also available to rent. Visitors can enjoy an authentic, chic escape—and the presence of a chef also guarantees a wonderful gastronomical experience.

OPPOSITE

The view from the swimming pool allows you to see how closely the renovation work followed the traditional Menorcan style—white-washed walls, olive green shutters, and terra-cotta roof tiles. The huge, one-thousand-square-meter building is split over three floors.

ABOVE

The cool and spacious summer living room is in a building adjacent to the house—the large iron-framed glazed doors letting in lots of light. Cane-line wicker armchairs and long benches scattered with cushions in bright fabrics by Élitis. The coffee table was made from a piece of natural wood by Carpintería Gavila in Mahón. Bamboo light fittings from Ay Illuminate.

FOLLOWING SPREAD

Somewhere between a British and an authentic Menorcan aesthetic, the winter dining room on the second floor uses muted tones, matching the original cement floor tiles. The walls are painted a lovely grey blue with verdigris woodwork. Vintage tables and chairs from El Recibidor, Barcelona, Shear ceiling light, Bert Frank.

BELOW

The garden-level living room space is bathed in light and furnished with vintage style pieces—sofa, chair, coffee table, and lamp from El Recibidor, and a stool in natural wood by Carpintería Gavila. A work by Catalan artist, *Paloma Pelaez entitled Bravo* (1958), hangs on the wall.

OPPOSITE

Gentle powder pinks and understated tiles in this first-floor bedroom. Atelier du Pont created a simple space with the white-washed built-in bed at the center of the immaculate room.

ABOVE
Adriana Meunié and Jaume Roig
place their creations side by side in
their home to see how they work
together. Adriana's piece, *Wool
Cloud*, made from the wool produced
by one of their sheep, hangs behind
Jaume's sculpture, *Organism*,
created from clay and wood.

40

Adriana Meunié and Jaume Roig

MALLORCA, SPAIN

Their creations can be found across the globe, featured in art biennials and galleries from Madrid to New York, passing by the London PAD fair—yet this couple chooses to live far away from it all. On a farm that stands alone in the Mallorcan countryside. The vaulted stable building is home to the showroom, while the former stalls host the studios. Adriana Meunié and Jaume Roig live a humble life surrounded by nature in their very own Noah's ark, among the ochre-coated stone walls and exposed beams, alongside a few chickens, two sheep, a dog, and a couple of peacocks.

Adriana left the stressful, brutal world of fashion to focus on her abstract art. Today, her studio is filled with virgin wool—collected from Mallorcan shepherds—raffia and armfuls of *carritx*, a type of grass that grows in the Balearic Islands. Adriana sews, weaves, braids, and blends the fibers that will become a piece of wall art, an organic canvas or an immense tapestry made from plants.

In the neighboring workshop, Jaume, a painter and ceramic artist, works the earth that has always been a part of his life: His mother was a ceramicist. His decorative, often totemic pieces are produced in series to be collected at will. His sculptural art with voluptuous shapes reminiscent of bottles is neither coated, nor glazed: The earth is left in its untouched state with natural colors and a matte finish. The palette of his canvas works oscillates between faux whites and almost blacks; organic shapes occupy a stunning, tranquil desert, a mental representation of a silent landscape when nothing remains.

LEFT & RIGHT
Adriana Meunié calls her work "textile paintings." Artwork that has volume, can be touched, and releases the scent of wool.

Jaume Roig is a native of Mallorca and adores the island. Be it ceramics, wood sculpting, or painting, he is a multifaceted artist whose works are permeated with local artisan practices.

LEFT

Adriana Meunié wears a coat she
made herself with the wool from
her sheep Joana. In the background,
a raffia on canvas composition.

A bouquet of natural fibers gifted to
Adriana by Jaume for her tapestries,
made up of alfafa and sisal rope.

ABOVE
This is the first artwork Adriana
Meunié and Jaume Roig created
together. The eight-meter-long
straw-and-clay landscape hangs in
the yoga room at Son Blanc Farmhouse in Menorca (see p. 58).

ABOVE

Iconic clay pieces by Jaume
Roig: *Stone* on the left and *Belly
Bottles* on the right. On the wall,
Weat Waves, raffia and linen on
canvas by Adriana Meunié.

In this installation, *Telluric Landscape*, by Jaume, a clay sculpture mounted on wooden legs
appears to be escaping from a lunar
painting on a canvas landscape.

OPPOSITE

A new example of the two artists'
joint work. The two ceramics,
Open Jaars, by Jaume stand
on wooden stools designed by
Adriana and made in Mallorca.
On the wall, woven sisal, alfa, and
carritx become *Waterfall Field*.

ART AT ITS HEART

MONTCLUS, FRANCE

PREVIOUS SPREAD
A large, four-hectare haven, the Mas Re.Source estate is covered with evergreen oaks, linden, olive, and cypress trees, creating an idyllic landscape. Mark Étienne and Rémy Coussedière added two separate houses to the old farm for visitors who want an immersive experience in nature.

OPPOSITE
Dry stone walls run the length of the large 20 × 4 m swimming pool. Marc and Rémy designed a pergola consisting of a steel structure—made by Olivier Vidal from L'art de fer in Saint-Quentin-la-Poterie—and pre-treated Douglas pine cladding to shade the teak daybeds.

An aesthetic landmark set just outside Cévennes, a far cry from the usual tourist excesses. Rémy Coussedière and Marc Étienne welcome us to their guest house, Mas Re.Source, and the inspirational visual and cultural dialogue between its old stones, restorative nature, contemporary photography, and designer furniture. It took over two years for the pair to transform an historic farm building into something boldly contemporary, working with architect Lucilla de Montis from DirectArchitecte. Rémy and Marc also called on landscape gardener Luc Échilley to enhance the outside spaces. "When we arrived here, the environment around the dilapidated building was completely wild," Marc explains. "Luc created an extraordinary garden, with the added bonus of it needing little in terms of water." The main building houses five light-filled suites. Every aspect has been completed to an exceptional standard—wide terraces, panoramic windows that make you feel as though you're teetering above the sky and completely at one with the landscape, and jaw-dropping bathrooms. The couple are art connoisseurs, and every space is an opportunity to display their amazing photography collection, amassed over thirty-five years. "Our art is the nerve center of our farm," Rémy confirms. "We want to create interactions between contemporary style and the past, but the photography is always the starting point, the springboard. That's where our inspiration comes from; the materials, objects, and furniture follow."

Two separate houses for guests, each with bold features, were built nearby. One is stone, the other is wood. Each has a living room, kitchen area, bathroom, and stunning views. Lower down, the panoramic swimming pool looks right out over the Cèze Valley and Mount Ventoux. You can lose hours sitting under the pergola and drinking in the view. Around candlelit tables in the evening, you'll enjoy meals cooked by Marc using fresh, local ingredients—and become completely enchanted by this special way of life.

RIGHT
A few meters from the main building, the two separate houses blend perfectly into their surroundings, with sweeping views across the valley and the Mount Fuji–like atmosphere of Mount Ventoux in the distance.

Architect Lucilla de Montis of
DirectArchitecte designed the two
fifty-square-meter houses to be resolutely contemporary, but in different
styles. The first has a wood frame
and is clad in pretreated Douglas
pine; the second house is in stone
and built from cinder blocks. It is
covered in local stone found on-site.

FOLLOWING SPREAD
The dining room is set in an old
stable and retains a rustic air: with
ancient, exposed stone and terra-
cotta briquettes on the floor and
partway up the wall. The briquettes
were made by hand at Les Terre
Cuites d'Aizenay, a family business operating for 150 years which
has been awarded EPV *Entre-
prise du Patromoine Vivant* distinc-
tion (Living Heritage Company).
Vintage chairs from a Barjac
antiques fair are arranged around
two three-meter teak tables. Rémy
and Marc made the lights that
illuminate the ensemble from
different sized filament bulbs.

ABOVE
The cathedral-like living room of
the wooden house is one of the
features of the renovation, bathed
in light from a huge window made
by metalworker Olivier Vidal.
La Photocopieuse (The Photo-
copier), a major work comprising
forty-two photographs, by artist
Julien Bernard is on display here.
The room is furnished with vintage
pieces, mainly items found at Barjac
antiques and flea markets. A set
of three lights, Bubble by George
Nelson, hangs from the ceiling.

OPPOSITE

In suite C5, located upstairs in an old barn, the yellow on the walls is Bivouac (Hypnotik), creating a backdrop for three photographs from the *Windows* series by Belgian artist Luc Dratwa. They contrast with the bedside tables made from old beams reclaimed from the original farm.

ABOVE

In their private living room, Marc and Rémy tiled an entire wall in Lume tiles in Musk, Marazzi. Untitled monotype (resin and pigments) by artist Gérard Traquandi (2011). In the foreground a 1960s Scandinavian table from a Barjac fair. The wood and steel stairway was designed by Lucilla de Montis and made by metalworker Geoffrey Faure. A large kudu head is displayed on the wall, found in Deyrolle, Paris. The floor is sanded concrete screed.

ABOVE

The wall in the light-filled garden suite is painted green, *Secret des druides* by Hypnotik to emphasize the two framed prints, *Humanity Man 01:27am* and *Humanity Women 02:22am*, by artists Lucie de Barbuat and Simon Brodbek. The baskets collected during travels in Egypt subtly complement the embroidered cotton cushions, CFOC.

OPPOSITE

For the huge twenty-three-square-meter C4 suite Rémy and Marc wanted to create a spectacular, theatrical bathroom with a large platform and double shower. The floor, walls, and ceiling are travertine. The washbasin unit was created from an olive tree trunk found on-site. Set of three vases were found at Barjac.

A RURAL AESTHETIC

MENORCA, SPAIN

PREVIOUS SPREAD
Completely renovated by architectural studio Atelier du Pont to create an enchanting hotel, the imposing traditional farmhouse sits in a gorgeous agricultural setting. The gardens created by landscape architect Eugenia Corcoy de Febrer run all the way down to the Mediterranean Sea, populated by olive trees and dotted with pathways linking the various buildings.

OPPOSITE
An elegant living room provides guests with a warm welcome beneath the *finca*'s vaulted ceilings that were skilfully restored by local artisans. The rough stones, large jute rug by Élitis, solid oak and straw armchairs and *radassier*, by Midi Éditions, and the ceramic side tables that were handmade in Portugal at Flores Textile Studio, all work beautifully together.

Husband-and-wife team Benedicta Linares Pearce and Benoît Pellegrini collaborated with Paris-based architecture studio Atelier du Pont to take a traditional farm and its magnificent estate on the island of Menorca and create Son Blanc Farmhouse. Son Blanc is a conscientious luxury hotel that favors the use of natural materials and artisanal expertise, a harmonious balance between the environment and human ingenuity. At an individual level, working against climate change requires time and reflection and it took six years for this project by Menorcan Benedicta and her French partner, Benoît, to come to fruition, in association with Atelier du Pont.

Architect Anne-Cécile Comar and her team worked with the two existing buildings: the main *finca* and an old barn, or *boyera*, on a wonderful 130-hectare estate of olive trees, oak forest, valleys, and rocks looking out over the Mediterranean. The focus on environmental considerations and self-sufficiency influenced the architectural decisions—the project features solar panels, geothermal heating, natural air conditioning, and reclaimed wood. Everything from the design to the expertise of the Menorcan artisans is in perfect alignment. This is apparent in a design where space is given priority—from the communal areas to the fourteen bedrooms and suites. Unsurprisingly, there's a focus on sourcing locally; ecological materials like Marés sandstone, whitewash, wild olive wood, terra-cotta, clay, and linen are all part of the textural interchanges and the blend of materials and bespoke pieces created for each space by local artists. It is a regenerative deep dive into beauty, rustic life, and art.

RIGHT
A few lucky guests can enjoy a suite with a private terrace set with Ethimo furniture and an Élitis rug. It's the perfect spot to enjoy a moment of repose in the shade of olive trees beneath a turquoise sky.

FOLLOWING SPREAD
Today, the *boyera*, or old barn, houses the restaurant, bar, kitchens, and a large event space for weddings and activities like yoga and meditation. The terraces face the sea and are protected from the sun by a set of shades by La Scourtinerie in Nyons, France (see pp. 70–73). The enchanting surroundings are scattered with gauras, pink grasses, and mastic trees.

ABOVE & OPPOSITE

In the hallway, Atelier du Pont retained the vaulted design and created a magnificent organically curved stairway. The pair of sculptural chairs and table were made to order in burnt beech by joiner Vincent Vincent. On the table, artisan-made wood-fired vases by Pretziada in Sardiana. Aurea and Ares natural rattan plinths by Heaps & Woods stand in the background. The doorframe and window frame were made from reclaimed oak from a Spanish monastery by Carpintería Gavila in Mahón. The floor is Marès sandstone.

The table in the elegant, light-bathed breakfast room was made by Carpintería Gavila in Mahón, from reclaimed oak from a Spanish monastery. The floor is Marés sandstone. Cadieras chairs in oak and natural straw, Midi Éditions. The soft felt lampshade by Vacht Van Vilt seems to float above a ceramic dinner set, designed for Son Blanc by potter Isaac Femenías Ferrà.

In a large living room upstairs, the chimney is Marès sandstone with fluted plaster on the surrounding walls. The wall lights were made by potters at the Danidevito Studio and designed by Atelier du Pont. The Palma sofa by Pierre Frey is flanked by two chairs—Margas and Fly, &Tradition. The Clara stool is carved teak from Heaps & Woods. Burnt wood carved coffee table, Lucas Castex; vases, Midi Éditions.

A wonderful view out to sea from the restaurant's sizable terrace in the *boyera*. Meals here are created using local produce and include regional specialties, served in the shade of olive trees. Genoa chairs, TrabA.

ABOVE
In one of the three bedrooms with
an abundance of textile decorations,
the wall displays a braided cotton
work by the Cañadas Murúa studio.
A bedside table either side, chamotte
lamps designed by Atelier du Pont
and made by potter Núria Efe.

In each suite, the architects have
designed custom headboards,
made by local artisans in a variety
of materials (wood, terra-cotta,
fabric). This one, decorated with
terracotta tiles inspired by Venetian blinds, and made by Ceràmica
Cumella in Barcelona, separates
the bedroom from the bathroom.

OPPOSITE
A small separate annex has been
restored with its original natural
feel in mind and turned into a suite.
The superb bathroom features a
stone bathtub that was made in
situ. Wooden stool, Polspotten.

ABOVE
The muted autumnal shades of
the *scourtins* are created on-site
in Nyons by Tijani Aouraghi, the
partner of Sophie Villeneuve Fert,
who is a descendant of the founder.

70

La Scourtinerie

NYONS, FRANCE

Scourtin filters have long been used to press oil from olive paste. It was Ferdinand Fert who, in 1892, invented a revolutionary weaving machine to produce these natural fiber filters; the very first machine to weave round shapes has been used ever since, working with solid, rotproof coconut fiber. Success was inevitable and for decades the oil produced at Drôme (Nyons) and beyond would be pressed using these *scourtins*. But things changed in the 1950s when the historic winter frost of 1956 saw the olive trees perish, and the Algerian War that impacted French commerce, causing mills to close, put the business in peril. Ferdinand's son, Georges Fert, had the lifesaving idea to repurpose production and make *scourtins* for use as rugs and mats.

The old silk farm is still used today for production; nylon filters that meet today's food production standards for oil and wine are woven here, as are traditional *scourtins* for use as decorative objects like table mats, doormats, and round or oval rugs measuring up to two and a half meters in diameter.

Since 2017 a further business idea has brought renown to La Scourtinerie: the fabrication of coconut sail shades. Their woven texture allows air to pass through and create a gentle breeze. It has been hugely successful with both private customers and public places. The sail shades have been developed by Arnaud Fert, the worthy heir to a line of visionary and creative entrepreneurs.

RIGHT
These spare bobbins come direct from Kerala in southern India and arrive already dyed; the heaped skeins are dyed on-site.

Some sail shades hung at the entrance of La Scourtinerie. Woven from rotproof, resistant coconut fiber, they diffuse the light and allow air to flow. A lovely example at Son Blanc, in Spain (see p. 62).

You can create your own bespoke
scourtin by choosing your colors
and the widths of the rings. Clients
often send La Scourtinerie their
designs, along with a photo of
where the rug will be placed.

Sophie Villeneuve Fert represents
the fifth generation of this creative
and entrepreneurial family. Here
she operates the weaving machine
that was patented in 1892 by her
grandfather, Ferdinand Fert.

A winding machine turns skeins into
bobbins ready for weaving. Orange,
brick-red, tilleul, gray, and brown;
the debate over whether bright colors
or soft colors are best continues . . .

THE PERFECT PLACE TO PERCH

CORSICA, FRANCE

PREVIOUS SPREAD
For this home perched above the scrubland, architect Thomas Fourtané of Archipetrus decided on a mixture of different woods: red cedar is used on the exterior cladding and roof tiles, ipe for the balconies, and Douglas pine for the brise-soleil. Sitting above a superb beach with crystal waters, every bedroom looks out onto the Mediterranean through large windows.

OPPOSITE
The walkways and balconies mean the whole family can enter the rooms from the outside. Hidden behind the holm oaks, strawberry, juniper, olive, and mastic trees, it's like living inside a protective bubble.

This wooden building was designed via a collaboration between the agencies Archipetrus and L'Agence No. 15. Located in southern Corsica, the structure is in perfect harmony with the surrounding landscape. The views are breathtaking—on one side the vacation home with the sea lapping below, and green mountains on the other. Blocks of sculptural eroded granite sit on the sand like pieces in a giant dice game, making the location even more spectacular.

The living room sets the tone with views out over the sea and the horizon. It was designed by Claire Euvrard from interior design studio L'Agence No. 15 in Paris. The space is devoid of clutter with the walls painted blue in contrast with the natural wood used on the exterior, evoking a "cabin-chic" feel. She carefully describes the first stages of the project: "When I started to think about the layout of the house, a giant sea snail came to mind—a curved wall unfurls between the hallway and the living room to section off the kitchen appliances. There's something convivial about its roundness." This main room is the nerve center of the house, a place where family and friends meet. "The build's main challenge was to successfully transform while maintaining the same dimensions," adds Claire. "The structure is based on a house built in 1973 and we're in a protected area."

Architect Thomas Fourtané from Archipetrus agency in Porto-Vecchio focuses on ensuring harmony and balance between the home and its environment on all his projects. With this design he concentrated on evoking a sense of free movement through the interplay of walkways and terraces that lead to the four bedrooms (there are another three at garden level). The views are extraordinary here, too. "It was natural to orientate them towards the beach," he adds.

RIGHT
Looking out over the sea and swathes of pink gauras flowers, the primary bedroom enjoys plenty of light. On the bed, washed linen sheets by La Redoute Interiors and a linen throw by Maison de Vacances. In the corner, 1960s wooden chairs, found on the premises, and African masks from the Paul Bert Serpette market in Saint-Ouen. Rattan outside chair from the Saint-Ouen flea markets, and sage linen cushions by Linge Particulier.

BELOW

A wonderful spot for dining beneath a wood-and-reed pergola near the pool, set against a beautiful backdrop of olive trees and holm oaks.

OPPOSITE

The ever-present sea can be seen from the stunning 14 m × 4 m infinity pool. Swimming through the blue water, it's like you're floating high with the sea below and the foliage all around—yellow curry plants, santolina, and strawberry trees.

ABOVE

Looking onto the terrace, the large living room pairs blue with terracotta. Sofa cushions, Élitis and La Redoute Interiors. A Cross/Nepal mineral resin coffee table by Janine Vandebosch for Interni Édition sits on a Toulemonde Bochart rug. Ino Mobilier at Porto-Vecchio vases and mugs, Polspotten natural wood stools. On the right, a Cala wood and rope outside chair. The understated corner fireplace was designed by Claire Euvrard.

OPPOSITE

The dining area is adjacent to the kitchen and opens onto the garden. The two long storage benches were designed by the interior architect and are covered by seat pads and plain linen cushions from Merci and La Redoute Interiors, patterned cushions by Élitis. The bespoke table is made from solid walnut with black painted steel legs; it measures 3.5 m × 1.1 m. Babila chairs, from Pedrali, and Cana light fitting from Kreon. Polspotten carafes are displayed on the shelves.

The huge ipe wood terrace in front of the lounge has everything you need. The simple layout features benches designed by Claire Euvrard with tobacco linen cushions from Haomy. The concrete-and-teak coffee tables are by Tribù: the perfect response to the three 1965 C317 poly-ethylene-and-steel chairs by Japanese designer Yuzuru Yamakawa, reissued by Feelgood Designs. The fish trap light on the floor is from La Maddalena in Sardinia.

OPPOSITE
The height of the living room ceiling is 4.6 meters up to its frame. Its walls and ceiling are painted with HC57 Pale Medici Blue by Ressource, evoking the Mediterranean Sea. The hanging shelves are from Made.com and the Chimbarongo lights are from PET Lamp. The door, designed by the interior designer, matches the oak battens on the wall separating the kitchen from the hallway.

BELOW
A rounded partition wall conceals some of the kitchen, introducing a feeling of delicateness to this large space. The central island features white painted storage units and a granite countertop. The lighting by Ay Illuminate plays with the transparency of the materials used.

A SUNNY RETREAT

MYKONOS, GREECE

PREVIOUS SPREAD
Studio Block722 designed the swimming pool with its endless views of the sea and nearby islands; wide resin steps make it easy to slip into the water. A comfortable outside room was created with sweeping views, shaded by a covering of dried palm leaves.

OPPOSITE
Everything in this room has been made to measure from the architecture studio's sketches. A beautiful idea in the main bedroom: an artisan-made wood-and-rope headboard. A palette of gentle blues with AM.PM linen sheets, a honeycomb bedspread by Vivaraise, and natural linen cushions found in Athens. The rug and bedside table were sourced on the island; Flos light.

The architect duo from Athenian studio Block722 wanted to create a refuge shaped by the harsh beauty of the wild coast, far removed from party nights and packed beaches. A contemporary architectural response with a deep connection to an exceptional site where the Aegean Sea rules and being able to get away from it all is a given. Located in Alemagou—"the end of the world" in Greek—the house avoids all the usual Cycladic clichés. Traditional rounded shapes give way to sharp, minimalist edges that echo the environment. The considered, pared-back style emphasizes the majesty of the landscape, the deep blue of the sky, and the sea: It's as though every line is designed to blend with the elements.

Founded by talented duo Sotiris Tsergas and Katja Margaritoglou, Studio Block722 brings together Mediterranean and Scandinavian influences. "We spend our lives between Greece and Sweden, which inspired us to pinpoint a balance between the two cultures. The Cyclades lend themselves perfectly to Scandinavian minimalism, don't you think?" asks Sotiris. It's a philosophy expressed in the refined elegance of this project—somewhere between Nordic precision and the warmth of the South. The interior of the house is a continuation of this vision; floors are smooth concrete, walls are whitewashed, furniture is designed by Katja and made to order in Greece, alongside Portuguese rugs and other carefully curated items. Wood, linen, and metal rub shoulders to create subtle contrasts, seen in the monumental lights in the kitchen above tables made from ancient elm. Even the door handles from Japan are testament to exceptional attention to detail.

This house created for friends stands isolated and alone, just a stone's throw from the clear water, forever deep in conversation with nature. The architecture of the house doesn't dominate but rather soothes and enhances the harsh beauty of Mykonos.

RIGHT
A place where family and friends passing through can gather, the swimming pool is in a perfect spot. The many daybeds around this haven of blue are the ideal place to laze.

OPPOSITE

Every part of the rooftop terrace looks out over the Aegean Sea. This is a quiet place to enjoy being alone and breathtaking views. The architects installed a rope shade tied across a wooden structure to create plays of light.

FOLLOWING SPREAD

Architects Sotiris Tsergas and Katja Margaritoglou designed a built-in banquette for the living room, covered by a natural linen seat cushion by Nikos Haritos. The bespoke interior oak shutters installed in this huge, understated room provide welcome shade. Coffee table, Mos Design and low stool by Vivaraise.

ABOVE

Beneath a pergola, the summer dining room features an oak table by Studio Block722. The light was made locally, echoing the play of sunlight against the wall.

ABOVE

Through a whitewashed arch, the kitchen blends sleek lines and elegance. The architects designed the understated solid oak central island and cupboards. The Corian® countertop echoes the polished concrete floor.

OPPOSITE

The dining room is adjacent to the kitchen and furnished with a solid oak table and two braided wicker benches designed by Block722. Embroidered cushions from Mille et Claire, Hans Wegner and Carl Hansen chairs, glass lights from Bomma Lights.

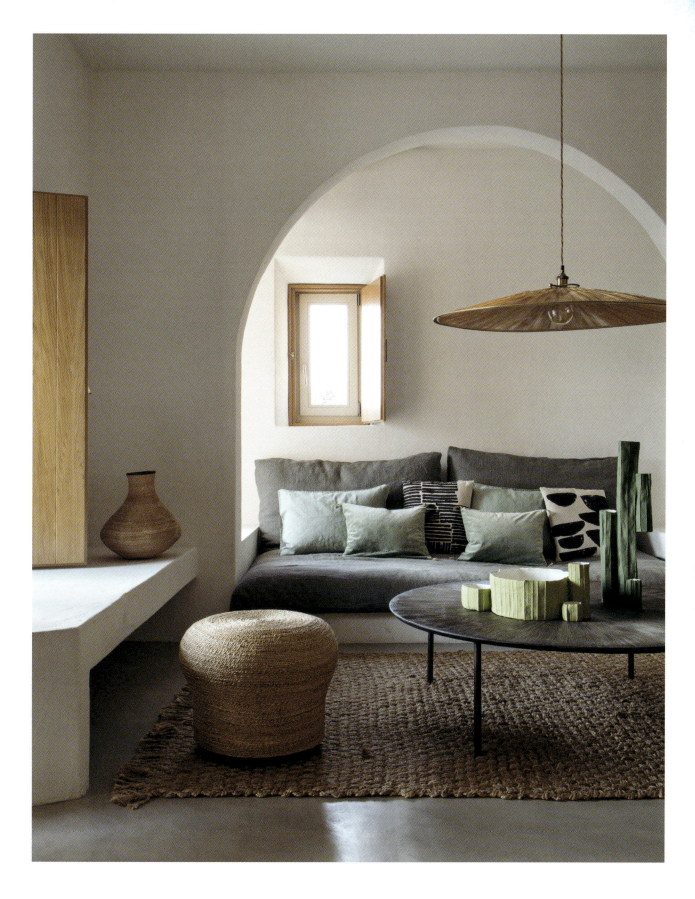

OPPOSITE
The large summer kitchen and
dining room are set within the sloping terrain and enjoy shade from
a pergola of hazel wood. Generously wide made-to-measure
daybeds surround the pool.

ABOVE
An arch in one of the spacious
bedrooms provides space for a
seating area. The built-in banquette
is covered by seating pads and
cushions in washed natural linen.
On the Mos Design metal table,
paper pulp and clay vases by
Italian potter Paola Paronetto
(pp. 98–101). Rug by Vivaraise.

Paola Paronetto

PORDENONE, ITALY

Illusion can be seductive. At first you think you see layers of painted cardboard, fabric; maybe some crumpled paper, the light picking out its irregularities and folds. Paola Paronetto's unique pieces occupy a space at the intersection of art and design, offering a unique sensorial experience.

Textures are rough and matte, shapes irregular, in a rich palette of dark and pastel tones. Paola uses paper clay in a way that's unique to her. Paper clay is a mix of clay, paper paste, natural fibers (i.e., cotton and linen), and water. The mixture you get is easier to work with than traditional terra-cotta. The artist wanted to free herself from the traditional shapes you get from a potter's wheel. Paradoxically, she finds these too static. Her paper clay is flexible but solid. Accidents are allowed: the unexpected, the flaws that bring her bottles, bowls, and vases to life.

When asked who her favorite artist is, Paolo will say Alberto Burri. He turned the cracks and fissures of sun-dried mud into a rhythmic process. The bewitching palette used by Mark Rothko is another undeniable source of inspiration.

A vase by Paola Paronetto, liberated from its initial function, is prettier without flowers. It exists happily alone, or at the centerpiece of an ensemble like a Giorgio Morandi still-life arrangement. When Picasso made his vases, did he think they'd ever hold flowers?

BELOW
Paper clay pieces dry slowly in
front of the kiln. The clay mustn't
crack at this delicate stage.

LEFT
Paola Paronetto carefully brushes
away matter from each of her
creations until she obtains the
finish she wants. The "Ninfee"
series from her collection.

100

101

ABOVE
Composition of bowls and bottles
around a large Anémone bowl. The
raw material used to make each piece
and the delicacy with which they are
made has already proven irresistible to
several brands, leading to collaborations
with companies like Veuve Clicquot,
Piaget, Audemars Piguet, and Vipp.

THE HOUSE OF STRAW AND AZURE BLUE

COMPORTA, PORTUGAL

PREVIOUS SPREAD
Landscape gardener Charlotte Van Houtte designed the garden, which covers the entire length of the plot, creating a sense of depth. Its many essential plants make the walk up to the house a truly sensory experience. Built by architects Nuno Lopes and Nuno Carvalho, the main building sits alongside two "huts" with rice straw walls and thatched roofs that house the bedrooms. Outside, two 1930s Portuguese modernist chairs, Barracuda Interiors.

OPPOSITE
In the shadow of a tall pine, the swimming pool is laid with dark green tiles and blends effortlessly into the natural landscape. The tables and chairs in wrought iron and perforated fabric are by Barracuda Interiors from the 1960s. The Eurolax R1 fiberglass chaises longues by Charles Zubena for Club Med are from the 1970s. The Ceramic cockerel by José Franco is from the 2000s.

A house inspired by the ocean and surrounding natural environment emerges from rice fields and wild dunes in the Comporta region of Portugal. The building is bordered by seemingly endless beaches and plays with the idea of an idyllic fishing hut, evoking a desert island simplicity. Nuno Lopes was the architect for a build featuring a thatched roof and rice straw walls—local traditions and materials that embody a timeless local knowledge and expertise.

The shell and ocean fauna collections inside the house tell a heartfelt story—a response to the nearby Atlantic Ocean. Furnishings from 1960-1980 and Portuguese ceramics blend with the contemporary pieces expertly selected by the owner Alexandra, with the help of interior designer Alexandre Neimann of Barracuda Interiors in Lisbon. The result is a unique décor that is both eclectic and deeply organic. The dreamlike fresco by Redfield & Dattner in the dining room captures the spirit of Comporta, with subtle Surrealist references evoking the wild, poetic energy of the region.

This tranquil place is both unchanging and a product of its environment. "I discovered the site beneath the torrential rain of a storm in the middle of winter," explains Alexandra. "I was struck by the unique light, the magnificent rice fields, the storks perched on the chimneys and—more than anything—the sea whose power affected me deeply." She was captivated by this balance of harshness and beauty and decided it was the right place for her family home, a true vacation retreat. There's something magical about this timeless refuge where the song of the sea and the peaceful location combine to infuse each visitor with an instant sense of calm.

LEFT
Alexandra created a headboard from a 1950s rattan screen, Barracuda Interiors in Lisbon. The oak and ceramic tile bedside tables by Guillerme et Chambron are from the 1960s. The ceramic lamp by José Franco is from the 2000s.

The furniture, lighting, and artwork in the living room all relate effortlessly to one another. On the wall, a whale scapula and a large sawfish rostrum—marine pieces from Alexandra's private collection—and the tapestry *Cathédrale d'Arbres* (Cathedral of Trees) by Anne Laure, 1983. A Lindell & Co cushion is placed at the end of the 1970s sofa. A Bella Silva bowl, ceramic cockerel and Corail ceramic lamps from Barracuda Interiors arranged on top of a 1960s rattan coffee table by Paul Frankl. In the hall in the background, a 1950s rattan chair and ceramic Feuilles wall light by Barracuda Édition.

A superb fresco, created specially by the artist duo Redfield & Dattner, gives the large living space a unique ambiance. Colette Gueden 1960s chairs and *1725* Warren Platner Knoll armchairs surround the white wood Barracuda Édition dining table. Nuno Lopes designed the polished concrete central island and the kitchen cupboards, made by Nuno Carvalho's local team.

Here comes the sun. The ultra-relaxing outside living room features ingenious bamboo shutters to allow a cooling breeze through, as and when desired. Maison de Vacances cushions are generously piled on the built-in benches. The 1950s oak coffee table, pair of Moroccan rattan armchairs, shell chandelier, 1950s perforated metal chairs, and 1960s side table all contribute to the space's hippie chic vibe.

Alexandra opted for soft tones in her bedroom. The washed linen sheets chime with a wool blanket by Maison de Vacances and an Area natural fiber rug. Here, Barracuda Interiors, Lisbon, created a harmonious arrangement with the 1970s rattan chair, 1940s French ceramic wall light, and 1970s circular rug. A wooden bull in a popular local style from the beginning of the nineteenth century and a grog Bull lamp by Barracuda Édition sit atop a repainted nineteenth century console table.

In the living room, a 1950s table is ready for a chess game. Two large windows look out onto the surrounding nature and the ocean.

Each guest room opens onto a private terrace and the garden. Here, Alexandra chose natural, earthy tones, mixing furnishings and vintage pieces with textiles made from natural materials.

SUMMER ON THE SLOPES

LUBÉRON, FRANCE

PREVIOUS SPREAD
On the terrace, two teak tables ready
for family meals and parties are shaded
from the summer sun by a huge metal
pergola with reed panels by Marie-
Laure Helmkampf. The spaghetti
chairs and armchair were found on
Selency and give a lovely vintage
feel, set off by the dry stone walls.

OPPOSITE
Lower down, next to a terraced wall,
the swimming pool is surrounded
by a vast polished concrete poolside
area. Sheltered from the mistral, the
daybeds were made from salvaged
beams by talented cabinetmaker
Laurent Passe. The crochet para-
sols, sun cushions, and deck chairs
were sourced from Todo Bien.

Interior designer Marie-Laure Helmkampf worked with the proportions of an ordinary 1970s building in Lubéron in southern France to create it anew—with vast open spaces and a refined scenography. With vines, olive trees, and pine trees as far as the eye can see, the untouched magical landscape here is punctuated only by the rhythm of the mistral wind and the sound of cicadas. It's an irresistible place—which explains why two individuals in their thirties, captivated by the three-hectare plot, chose to start from scratch. Their goal? To introduce beauty into the building and bring it back to life. They erased every trace of the dated original building, choosing to prioritize light, sleek lines and raw materials like wood and stone. With the challenge set, the charmless old building was transformed into a stunning destination.

"It was a boring house with gloomy, rather poky spaces," explains Marie-Laure. Architect Rudy Flament opened and extended the exterior toward the Mediterranean garigue. Meanwhile, Marie-Laure completely remodeled the interior by opening up the space, installing sliding doors and a single-story concrete stairway to introduce a quasi-industrial, loft-style feel. The plentiful use of wood is the work of Laurent Passe (see pages 124–129), a cabinetmaker specializing in upcycling who enjoys experimenting with different finishes—natural, burnt, and painted—to decorate and give soul to a space.

An appreciation of local craftsmanship is central to the project. Prominence is given to high-quality, antique materials from the neutral bedrooms to the living room—which elegantly pairs vintage items with custom sofas. "I sourced lots of vintage pieces for an authentic feel," explains the interior designer.

If it feels as though this farmhouse has always been here, the simple décor and its close relationship to nature are reminders that its owners lived in Japan and are believers in Lao Tzu's philosophy of emptiness: "It is not the clay that makes the pot, but the emptiness inside that makes it useful."

RIGHT
The light-filled living room has
large ironwork windows opening
out onto the garden and terraces
of this Provençal home. This is a
place for relaxing, either on the two
comfortable bespoke wooden sofas
by Atmosphère & Bois, or on the
original 1950s Wim Rietveld Oase
armchairs, sourced on Selency.

In the kitchen designed by Marie-
Laure Helmkampf and Laurent
Passe, wooden varnished elements
are paired with a natural stone
countertop and kitchen sink.

BELOW

The summer kitchen is close to the pool, with a central island designed by Marie-Laure Helmkampf and made by Laurent Passe using recycled wood. You can perch on a tall stool here whenever you want to enjoy a snack. The structure sits on drystone pillars with a roof made of solid beams and old Provençal wood from Comps. The light fitting was bought in L'Isle-sur-la-Sorgue.

OPPOSITE

Enjoyable contrasts between the pared-back poured concrete staircase, designed by the interior architect, the simple whitewashed stone walls, and the old cellar door, sourced from a garage sale. A papier-mâché–plaster bowl and vintage glassware by Pascale Saint-Sorny are displayed on top of an old workbench found in a Saint-Dionisy flea market.

FOLLOWING SPREAD

The spacious wood and stone kitchen was designed by Marie-Laure and made by Laurent. The central island features original old beams and a gray natural stone countertop with integrated cooking appliances. The fronts of the storage units and fridge were made from planks from old carriages, untouched or painted white. The artisan-made iron and glass double doors lead out onto a terrace overlooking the estate.

OPPOSITE

The bathroom in the garden-level main bedroom is set on a concrete platform, with the headboard cleverly separating the two spaces. Old beams surround the bed, which is made up with bronze-colored Lissoy linen sheets.

ABOVE

In the bathroom area, a wash-stand on a wooden base sits against the black polished concrete wall, enjoying a superb view over the garden through a huge ironwork window. The bamboo towel rack is by La Maison Pernoise and the black taps are Fantini.

FOLLOWING SPREAD

The house and its extensions are covered entirely in dry stone, set on terraces created on the sloping terrain by landscape architect Chris Van Loock of Hortus. The ground-level twenty-five-meter pool is edged by polished concrete and resin, with sumptuous daybeds created out of old beams by Laurent Passe.

OPPOSITE

Bleached and burnt, the wood used in this kitchen comes from oak floorboards from an old merchant carriage. Laurent Passe made the central island. Part of the workshop is set aside for metalwork; the countertop is a slim sheet of steel sourced elsewhere. Paper lighting from Saint-Sorny.

Laurent Passe

BEAUCAIRE, FRANCE

From the moment you enter the workshop, you can smell the aroma of the Ventoux cedar planks. Freshly delivered, this batch is destined to be turned into huge tables. A little farther along, pieces of a future kitchen in burnt wood are ready for delivery to a house in Solonge. On the mezzanine, hundreds of old doors and planks lie drying under the dust and spiderwebs.

As a child, Laurent Passe would collect bits of wood that his grandfather would transform into toys. And from a young age his father, an antiques expert, showed him the beauty of objects and materials. Armed with a carpentry qualification, and later, some wood sculpture lessons, he threw himself into the construction of a house of stone. Almost immediately he started a business dealing in reclaimed wood and doors; buying, selling, restoring. . . . Nothing could stop him, even the devastating Rhone floods of 2002 and 2003, which destroyed his stock and ruined years of hard work.

His current showroom opened in Beaucaire in 2012. Here, Laurent aims to bring out the soul of the wood, to tease out its vibrancy and jagged shape. He only works with reclaimed wood: bits from old rail carriages, beams and floorboards from old barns, shelving from an old shepherd's hut that still carries the marks of the cheese rounds it once held. Full of history and energy, frequently saved from destruction, it's alive and destined for a wonderful future. This bleached, dried, burnt, oiled, painted, and natural wood will go on to create beautiful, joyful kitchens and festive tables. Laurent says, "I'm interested in the energy you can introduce into a space, the emotion you feel when you touch a material."

RIGHT

You can't pigeonhole Laurent. He is a cabinetmaker, yet he also plans and makes kitchens and interiors, designs and crafts tables, drawers, closets, and desks. And he works with metal and stone, too. First and foremost an artisan, the designer reveres beautiful materials.

PAGE 126

Two thousand old doors are stored in Laurent Passe's workshops and warehouses; they need to be kept well-stocked to be able to quickly respond to the needs of architects and clients.

PAGE 127

Burnt wood closet made from oak from an old merchant carriage, with a steel base and leather handles. Simply planed, the niche is from the same batch of wood.

LEFT
Arranged on a burnt pine console table made from floor-boards from an old barn, *raku yaki* pottery from Saint-Quentin-la-Poterie. After scorching, the wood is oiled to help it stabilize.

LEFT
Oak beam oval Psyché table. "The trees are waiting to be read," wrote Francis Ponge.

ABOVE
The Roch chest of drawers is made from a block of granite; its drawers are supported by an invisible steel structure. They are made from old shelving that was used to hold cheese. The moss was collected from the Bois de Païolive and sewn onto the baize.

OPPOSITE
Laurent designed an unusual head-board for a project in Lubéron in Provence, also from old carriage boards. The wood was burned using a large blowtorch. The challenge was to stop the material from curving while it was being warmed.

ABOVE
Edged by cacti and old, low
stone walls, the estate sits under
a perfect sky, as though part of
a René Magritte painting.

OPEN SPACES

PUGLIA, ITALY

PREVIOUS SPREAD
An old farmhouse, or *masseria*, Le Carrube has been transformed into a hotel for those in search of authenticity and enjoyment. Most of the rooms have a terrace or private garden.

BELOW
The captivating, timeless structure is a maze of pathways and walled gardens dotted with olive trees, inviting you to daydream for a while.

The rooms are decorated simply using original materials, with whitewashed arches and stone walls.

Le Carrube *masseria* nestles in the middle of the Itria Valley, protected by the welcome shade of ancient olive trees. The former farming property sits on a landscape bathed by the sea and dried by the wind. From a distance, its high walls and immaculate towers make a picture-perfect scene that's impossible to resist.

You reach the whitewashed buildings, with their simple verdigris window frames, via a huge central courtyard. Visitors enter through a beautifully understated hallway. The air under the large vaults is cool and the brickwork benches scattered with cushions invite you to stop and relax a while.

Marisa Melpignano appears, the owner of the property, and she's rightly proud of the magnificent renovation. The founder of the Masseria San Domenico, her determination has once again enabled her to preserve the charm of an authentic Masseria while subtly adding discreet, high-performance hotel elements into the mix. Le Carrube is located a few kilometers from the whitewashed town of Ostuni and beaches of the Adriatic Sea. It sits at the end of a winding track that takes you through active farms and olive tree fields strewn with scarlet poppies.

The property is made up of nineteen bedrooms and suites, two dining rooms, a bar, two swimming pools, patios, and numerous terraces, dominating the spectacular landscape. It's an environment that champions simplicity, where to take time to relax is a way of life and the day floats by like the clouds in the bright blue sky. If you want to take a stroll, you can discover the labyrinthine estate on foot with its original *trullo*. The sea is close, too, with coves edged in turquoise. Here, you can enjoy the sun until its last rays fade and dinner calls. Then you can sit and enjoy a largely vegetarian meal made from local, seasonal produce and—true to the principles of the Mediterranean diet—some good wine from Pouilles.

OPPOSITE

Large tables sit beneath cooling pergolas and climbing vines, ready for a glass of lemonade, made by the *masseria* staff using fruit from the kitchen garden. A pleasant contrast to the verdant surroundings, the buildings are whitewashed, as is the tradition in the Pouilles region. Interior courtyards and terraces: Nooks offer spots to enjoy the welcoming calm of the space.

FOLLOWING SPREAD

On arrival at Carrube, you are greeted by an idyllic meadow of poppies and wildflowers. The Adriatic Sea shimmers on the horizon.

OPPOSITE

A tricky choice: You have two
swimming pools to choose from
at the center of the renovated
farm. The pools are surrounded
by stones and give the appearance of having been there forever.

ABOVE

Breakfast can be taken in a variety of
spaces. Green tables by Ethimo are
placed in the courtyards and gardens,
allowing the restorative, nurturing
effects of the sun to be fully enjoyed.

DELICATE MATERIALS

BLAUZAC, FRANCE

PREVIOUS SPREAD
The 350-square-meter farm was renovated from top to bottom; today its stand-out features include a superb garden planted with grasses, olive trees, and pines, and a swimming pool laid with dark green tiles. The pool decking in Massaranduba wood, made by Jean-Jacques Michaux is home to AM–PM daybeds adorned with Mapoésie sarongs.

OPPOSITE
An old barn houses the vast, sun-drenched living room. Martial and his father, Jean-Jacques, tiled the whole space in Terres Cuites de Raujolles stone tiles with the spectacular chimney breast as a focal point. Lights from Les Affaires Étrangères in Uzès hang above the two bespoke Bed & Philosophy natural linen sofas.

This enormous wine-producing farm perched high up in the village of Uzège has been infused with modern comfort, through a light-filled scenography. The design by an experienced creative team melds contemporary style with Provençal simplicity. "When we visited the farm, inhabited by the same family for generations, we were completely gripped by the stories that unfolded as you passed from room to room," explains Martial, one of the two owners. "We immediately saw how we could allow the story to continue by bringing in a contemporary vision that didn't try to cover over the wrinkles of the past that make the house so unique. We found it in poor condition, some of the spaces at the property still had their original clay floors—along with a pigsty, stables, haylofts, outbuildings, wine cellars, and more."

New plans for the use of space on the first floor were quickly put in place. Communal living spaces are simply organised around a huge living room in an old barn—a space for getting together that opens into the kitchen and garden. Martial was well-versed in what needed to be done and began the meticulous renovation alongside successful entrepreneur Jocelyn Descazaux and supported by his father, Jean-Jacques Michaux—a passionate joiner. "We skillfully introduced some more radical elements like opting for polished concrete for floors, staircases, and bathrooms, bespoke metal framework, a huge terracotta tile chimney in the main room, and a high-performance kitchen." In contrast to the vast living room downstairs, the eight bedrooms on the second floor were designed as cozy, intimate spaces with en suite bathrooms. Parents, friends, or children—there's a space for everyone at Mascal. In the morning, afternoon, and evening, everyone descends on the kitchen where tasty dishes are prepared, destined for the dining tables set up in the middle of the garden. Pines, oaks, cacti, grasses, a swimming pool, a boule court, and even the sound of crickets are here. It's clear keeping things simple sets the scene for making the most of life.

RIGHT
A series of rooms unfolds between the main living room and the entrance to the farm; the floors, walls, and ceilings play with common themes of earthy, ochre, and dark tones.

In the shade of the iron pergola covered in reeds, friends can enjoy wonderful meals on the reclaimed wood table designed by Martial and made by his father. The chairs were discovered in a Uzès bric-a-brac store, and the lights were found in the souks of Marrakech. The traditional Tamegroute crockery is from Les Affaires Étrangères.

PREVIOUS SPREAD
Adjoining the kitchen, the reading
room is decorated with a lime paint
(Havane by Ressource), highlighting
the original fireplace adorned with
a stunning paper applique piece by
Jean-Luc Mare (see pp. 150–153).
Martial made two comfortable
stone seats, adding seat cushions
and tobacco linen scatter cushions from Haomy. Cushions in
clay-colored linen from Maison de
Vacances and Havana cotton throw
from H&M Home. Carpet, Zara
Home; coffee table, Chabi Chic;
wooden side tables from the "Brick"
collection by Gervasoni. Ceramics
from Les Affaires Étrangères.

ABOVE
Martial made the striking chimney
place and layout by hand with
terra-cotta facings from Terres
Cuites de Rajoulles that perfectly
match the natural clay lamp and
the wood and rope armchair
from Les Affaires Étrangères.
The linen curtains provide some
welcome coolness during the
heat of the summer months.

OPPOSITE
The materials in the kitchen-diner
relate beautifully to one another—
1959 Panton chairs by Verner
Panton surround the wooden table
by Jean-Jacques Michaux, and the
concrete island features green
ceramic tiles (Leroy Merlin). Here
and there pieces of pottery from
Les Affaires Étrangères echo the
tones of the original parefeuille
terra-cotta ceiling and the bare
stone walls. Light fittings from Ay
Illuminate add a quirky element
to the décor. Jean-Jacques made
the bespoke cupboard doors.

146

OPPOSITE

The understated main bathroom is decorated in mineral tones. The same polished concrete is used on the floor and walls to match the furniture and the washstand (an old *brasero*) made by Jean-Jacques Michaux, with a letter *M* feature for "Mascal"—the name of the farm. The Mita metal wire light fitting is from La Redoute and the ceramic stool is a Prisunic rerelease from Monoprix. On the wall, LED bulbs illuminate a large sheet of rock from behind, gently lighting the space.

ABOVE

The vaults and walls of the large main bedroom are painted in Foin by Ressource. Jean-Jacques made the bespoke oak doors for the closet and the headboard, adding some contemporary detailing. Linen sheets by Merci; bench and bull heads in black terra-cotta from Les Affaires Étrangères.

ABOVE
In the entrance to his workshop in
Sauve, a Millefeuille ceiling light
measuring one meter in diameter.
Jean-Luc Mares lamps can be viewed
by appointment; some are on display
at the Galerie Artwork in Uzès.

150

Jean-Luc Mare

SAUVE, FRANCE

After a career as a graphic designer in print advertising, Jean-Luc Mare has radically changed his relationship with paper. Leaving Paris for the shaded streets of Sauve in the Gard region of France, he founded a studio to create lights—or rather paper sculptures that seem to map an imaginary landform.

What is striking when we observe the artist's creative process is its apparent simplicity. The sheets of white paper (160 gsm) are drenched with a water spray, then scrunched firmly, as if being wrung out. Once unfolded, the sheets are ironed, which causes fine lines, cracks, and tiny perforations to appear; when these are lit, it seems as if we are looking at hills or ridgelines. Then comes the work of slicing the paper with a cutter to create half circles, squares, and other shapes; these designs are patiently layered and glued, one after the other, to create a stratified light. Smiling, Jean-Luc says that all he needs is an iron, a cutter, and a little glue to bring his creations to life.

Carefully folded and packed, the lamps travel easily because they are both lightweight and robust. Architects and individuals order directly from Jean-Luc; he works alone and has no desire to grow. "I don't want to become a factory." Each lamp resembles a landscape, evoking Japanese prints or the bluey outline of the Cévennes mountains on the horizon. Designer Isamu Noguchi once said, "We are a landscape of all we know."

BELOW
The designer cultivates a calm and serene working environment in which to execute his solitary craft.

Round Plune wall lights (a contraction of "pleine lune" meaning full moon) measuring 35, 50, 70, or 90 cm in diameter. Models of different sizes sit happily together on the same wall.

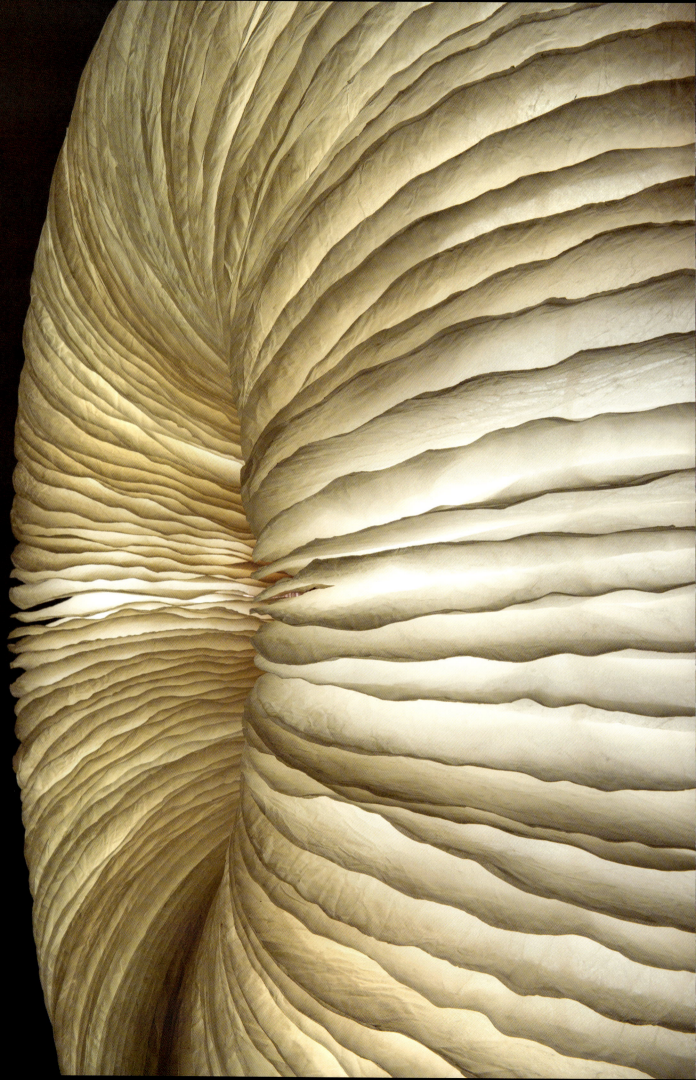

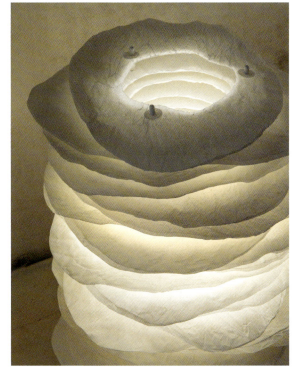

TOP LEFT
Iris wall light, diameter 130 cm. It is made up of fifty-eight paper "crepes," soaked, scrunched, ironed, cut, then glued together. This creation requires thirty hours of work.

ABOVE
These lamps are as beautiful extinguished as they are when lit. The extinguished lamp is a 180 cm prototype in its final stages. The lit lamp is the 50 cm diameter model of the Millefeuille lamp.

OPPOSITE
Detail from Iris light. Jean-Luc Mare sources his paper from Fedrigoni in Florence. He uses Pergamata Bianco paper for the cloudy whiteness, parchment finish, and strength. (see p. 145).

ABOVE LEFT
Millefeuille hirsuite lamp, 35 cm tall. Jean-Luc willingly evokes Ingo Maurer's Poul Poul lamp, itself an homage to the one created in 1924 by Poul Henningsen and Louis Poulsen.

AUGMENTED RADICALITY

GRÂNDOLA, PORTUGAL

PREVIOUS SPREAD
In the valley region of Alentejo, close to Grândola, the house designed by architect Gonçalo Bonniz emerges like a vessel built of glass, concrete, and wood. Its three wings run east to west. Its flat roof makes it melt into the environment, blending perfectly with the wild landscape dotted with holm oaks.

OPPOSITE
The color palette changes with the seasons in this vast and stunning landscape—arid in the summertime and carpeted with yellow flowers in the spring. The continual movement engenders a sense of inner peace, as you look on from the ipe wood poolside next to the gray concrete swimming pool.

This stunning house is tucked away in the valleys of the Alentejo and accessed via a dirt track. Its ultra-contemporary curves hug the surrounding landscape; a blend of traditional and cutting-edge materials on a monumental scale. The structure was designed by architect Gonçalo Bonniz to sit in perfect harmony with its environment, playing with concepts of transparency and concealment. Slate, exposed concrete, and wood are used to accentuate the immense thirty-five-meter run of windows, inviting a contemplative gaze.

The interior was designed by Emma Pucci and Valentina Pilia of Flores Textile Studio in Lisbon and features unique pieces by local artisans that demonstrate an unshowy mastery of natural materials. Alentejo itself is the inspiration for the palette here, ochre like the earth, the verdigris of the holm oak, ecru, and cream. Environmentally friendly, rustic materials were chosen in keeping with the location; flax from the garden, natural sheep wool, glazed pottery, a new take on traditional rugs from Arraiolos. "Our challenge was to use Portuguese expertise in a contemporary context," explain Emma and Valentina.

The space is largely open with a focus on interaction. The vast living area was designed to host family and friends; its clean lines encompassing two living rooms, a spacious kitchen, and an understated dining room. All six rooms in this large space walk a line between pared-back silhouettes and intimacy. It's a place where simplicity is in perfect balance with the demands of the building. Each season brings a new experience: meditative retreats in the spring, cooking courses in the summer, when the permaculture kitchen gardens are flourishing thanks to a spring discovered on-site. Eschewing excess in favor of the essential, reducing form so only the fundamental remains—all of a sudden time seems to just stop.

RIGHT
The house opens onto a mostly untouched natural environment. In front of the thirty-five-meter window the seventy-square-meter communal area enjoys a stunning panoramic view. A curved Pierre Augustin Rose sofa works well with a vintage coffee table from Galeria Bessa Pereira, Barcelona, and the pair of vintage armchairs from Barracuda Interiors in Lisbon. Pottery lamp, rugs, and stools by Flores Textile Studio.

PREVIOUS SPREAD
In the dining room, Karnak chairs and stools from e15 Design surround the large bespoke table by Flores Textile Studio. Lipari travertine and brass ceiling light from Garnier & Linker. In the background, a metal cabinet designed by Flores Textile Studio is decorated with a tapestry by deFio Rugs in Lisbon, alongside two locally made wooden chairs.

OPPOSITE
The huge functional kitchen occupies a space in the center of the living area. The nerve center of the house features a central island and large bespoke kitchen cupboards in Kebony Clear® wood.

BELOW
The reading area in front of a shuttered concrete fireplace features a vintage coffee table in blackened wood from Galeria Bessa Pereira and two vintage chairs, Barracuda Interiors. Wool rug, low stools, and cushions by Flores Textile Studio. The pottery collection displayed on the shelves has neutral tones and a matte finish, Raisin Ceramic in Lisbon.

The purity of line alongside the simplicity of local materials heightens the architectural aspects of every space.

FOLLOWING SPREAD
Flores Textile Studio cushions on the bespoke sofas in one of the two living rooms. Studio Mumbai armchair, Maniera gallery in Brussels, ceramic stools by Flores Textile Studio. Artwork is by Nicolas Lefeuvre, *Landscape Site 3*, from Jean-François Cazeau gallery in Paris.

PAGE 164
The use of neutral colors was an integral part of this project. Local slate and dark gray concrete influenced the materials chosen—warm Kebony Clear® wood is the perfect match for these tones, both inside and outside. Vintage wooden chair sourced in Lisbon.

PAGE 165
Gonçalo Bonniz selected materials that would blend into the surrounding landscape and withstand Alentejo's harsh climate. Concrete was chosen for the flooring and for the five-meter overhang that acts as a shade. For the façades, the architect opted for treated pine.

ABOVE
The six bedrooms are sparsely but boldly furnished and have access to the huge terrace that runs the length of the building. Waking up here is magical, with unforgettable views across the wild, valleyed landscape.

OPPOSITE
The whole bathroom opens onto a terrace shaded by a beautiful olive tree and bordered by vegetation. The view from the tub is wonderful.

A SPECIAL VIEW

COMPORTA, PORTUGAL

PREVIOUS SPREAD
Visitors arriving at this exceptional property are struck by the staggering view. The expanse of grasses shimmering in the wind was designed by landscape architect Louis Benech and reinterpreted by Alexandra de Csabay. At the top of the plot, the two buildings housing the lounge and the kitchen-diner look over the three buildings accommodating the suites.

OPPOSITE
Light plays across a wall in this outdoor lounge close to the bedrooms. Brickwork benches and two chairs designed in the 1920s by Robert Mallet-Stevens enjoy some welcome shade under the whitewashed wooden slatted roof.

It's hard to know where to look in this tranquil spot next to the water, edged with pine forests and dunes. The lush green rice fields, the grass dancing in the wind, or the houses that call to mind the fishing huts of yesteryear. The words of the Lisbon writer Fernando Pessoa come back to you, whispering, "During those hours when the landscape forms a halo around life."

Just outside Comporta, the outlines of a few houses emerge along boardwalk paths twisting and turning across the sand. The first building, at the top of the plot, is used for get-togethers and houses a combined living room and library. Separated by a huge terrace with an enchanting view, a second structure accommodates the kitchen-diner. The private suites are below, in the hollow of the rice fields; like sanctuaries for those who stay there, nomadic people who find themselves more easily through the very act of wandering.

Spatial design is paramount in the work of architects Clarisse Labro and Mark Davis of Labro & Davis, who have given the site an undeniably poetic feel. Precise words guide their work, "For the process to remain creative, you must always refer back to a project's original concept," explains Clarisse. "In this case the environment dictated what we needed to do, the slow, continual movement of the sand and the constant wind. It made sense for us to face the houses towards the dreamlike rice fields."

To perfect the idyllic environment, renowned landscape architect Louis Benech imagined a very graceful garden with lots of different plant varieties. "Louis successfully integrated the garden with the different buildings and created transitions by altering plants and textures," say the architects. The Atlantic Ocean rumbles against the sheltering dunes in the distance, magnifying the incredible beauty of the location.

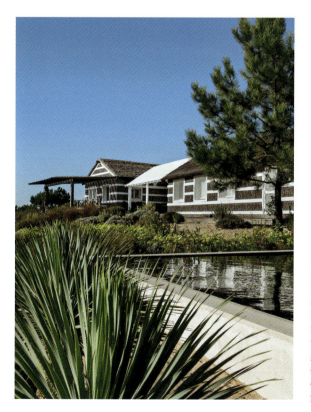

LEFT
The buildings were designed by architects Clarisse Labro and Mark Davis; they have thatched roofs, made from rice straw, and windows looking out onto the garden and the rice fields. An unendingly captivating view: indigenous plants and the swimming pool beneath a turquoise sky.

ABOVE
Lower down on the plot, wooden stairways close to the huts are concealed among the plant life so they vanish into the landscape. A small vintage rattan seating area is a tempting place to linger.

OPPOSITE
Water glitters in the sunlight. Running through the land-scape, canals edged by paths leading to a huge nearby beach.

172

The pool is lined with three tons of green tiles, perfect for a refreshing dip. It has a wonderful vista as far as the eye can see over the rice fields and the dunes. Louis Benech and Alexandra de Csabay planted a mixture of local plants around the pool including rock-roses, agave plants, yuccas, French lavender, and santolina.

OPPOSITE
A set of Danish chairs from Modernity in Stockholm with the 1960s solid elm table by Pierre Chapo in the dining room. Limited edition rug, Artek light fittings, Golden Bell by Alvar Aalto (1936). On the wall, Atelier Buffile ceramic plate, bull head discovered at antique dealer José Antonio de Brito Canudo, Santa Maria Velharis in Carvahal. Sideboard from Damien Tison Gallery in Paris.

ABOVE
The colors and materials work beautifully together in a bedroom. A plaited raffia headboard and bespoke curtains in brightly colored natural materials conceal a large dressing area.

The bathroom combines delicate colors with vintage pieces. The 1980 Prorok armchair, by Bořek Šípek for Driade; the wicker mirrors and rope wall lights are from Paul Bert Serpette antiques market; light fitting from the Jacques Grange et Pierre Passebon's Stork Club store in Carvahal.

FOLLOWING SPREAD
The garden occupies the space between the two main houses and the rice fields. The terrace is covered by a slatted, white-washed wooden roof, giving the area a luminous graphism. This is where the family enjoys meals at the metal table topped with black tiles by Mark Davis. 1950s Villa Cavrois chairs by Raoul Guys, Damien Tison Gallery, Paris.

OPPOSITE
Knitted wool and woolen fibers
intertwine, creating something
that's soft both in appearance and
touch. The ochre and black streaks
of the Sable du desert collection evoke the contrast between
the sun's light and shade.

Ghislaine Garcin

MARSEILLE, FRANCE

As soon as you see this wool, you want to touch it, to bring it to your cheek, feel the entwined fibers, sense their softness.

After a career in graphics and printing, Ghislaine Garcin moved into textile creation. She wanted to bring together two ancient techniques—felting and knitting. The former is obtained by pressing wool by hand with warm soapy water. It is during this mashing of fibers that the designer inserts pieces of knitting that then take root, graft themselves to the fibers, and meld with the felt. Incorporating these strips of knitting brings the graphic compositions to life: colored streaks, random shreds, broken stripes. The chosen palette is far removed from primary colors, and never bold; Ghislaine prefers muted tones, semi-colors, the understated combinations that plant dye offers today.

Combining felt and knitting in this way can create soft, comforting objects: seats and cushions, pots, mini-futons, meditation rugs—tactile creations that lend themselves to intimacy. Ghislaine takes inspiration from Japan; she has retained the art of living at floor level and the tenacious patience required for artisan work. A Nordic spirit also blows through her studio in Marseille, drifting in from countries where felt is a friend in formidable winters.

Basketry is a new field of experimentation for the designer: a simple sidestep from knitting to weaving, taken to explore new materials and movements.

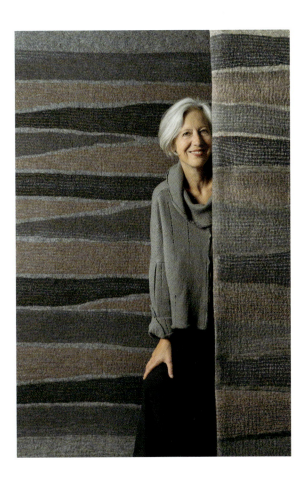

RIGHT
Ghislaine Garcin works with
both interior designers and individuals. Here, she poses in front
of a grey, brown, and pink rug,
which works happily as wall art.

OPPOSITE
Back to natural and soothing shades
with the Laine au carré range.

RIGHT
The Jardin zen line invites
contemplative meditation.
The soft materials and light
colors promote serenity.

ABOVE
With the Bleu des Calanques collection, the designer from Marseille
conjures the blue and green shades
of her Mediterranean roots.

The Tressages collection is the result
of a collaboration between Ghislaine Garcin and the basket maker
and artist Fabrice Serafino. The
plant dye by Lola Verstrepen works
wonderfully on woolen fibers.

183

TOUR OF THE TOWER

LOPUD, CROATIA

PREVIOUS SPREAD
A few kilometers from Dubrovnik, the splendid landscape on the island of Lopud looks across to the Adriatic Sea and the Elaphiti Islands. Architect Steven Harris and his husband, interior designer Lucien Rees Roberts, completed a total renovation of this sturdy defensive tower dating from 1460. It has been transformed into a vacation destination.

OPPOSITE
The kitchen is in what was originally the tower's water cistern. The majestic height of the original space has been retained, with a superb, vaulted ceiling and original walls dating from the fifteenth century. Simplicity itself, the long white oak table was designed by RRP, original Tulip chairs by Eero Saarinen, 1960, Knoll. The vintage Murano glass chandelier forms a centerpiece and was found in London.

New York couple Steven Harris and Lucien Rees Roberts enjoyed traveling the world before finally settling on the idea of renovating a ruined tower on a small island close to Dubrovnik. The transformation blends history, architectural heritage, and twentieth-century design masterpieces—all in one of the most dazzling settings in the Mediterranean. "The tower had amazing views," remembers Steven. "I've always been attracted to vertical buildings and their ability to control a landscape. There is a dialectic between the sense of refuge and prospect. But when we bought it, the only floor still intact was the stone-vaulted space housing the water cistern." Steven is an architect and Lucien an interior designer. They live in New York where their respective agencies are based—Steven Harris Architects and RRP (previously Rees Roberts + Partners).

Seigneurial is the word that comes to mind as you travel the winding country lanes, lined with oak and cypress trees swaying in the wind. There's not a car or house to be seen. Cicada song deafens from morning till night and the sea unfurls before you, hugging the hills and hamlets of the Dalmatian Coast. A designated historic monument, the tower first needed to be strengthened with concrete. Four floors were created on the fifteenth-century foundations: from the vaulted kitchen with robust stone walls at garden level right up to a huge living room on the top floor (where previous inhabitants would boil oil in the old fireplace to pour onto invaders).

Concrete, oak, ash, and metal interweave and blend with the original stone. "It isn't a strict historical renovation," Steven says. "More than anything, we wanted an interior that told a new story and mixed up different centuries." The furniture and artworks were chosen with an art collector's eye. Here, a dining table made from a jacaranda slab found in a house by Brazilian architect Oscar Niemeyer in Sao Paul; there, a pair of Charlotte Perriand armchairs and Pierre Paulin seats. Pieces by some of the most iconic designers of the twentieth century are ideal in this bold décor—in perfect harmony and enjoying a wonderful dialogue.

LEFT
Lucien designed the kitchen and its elegant contrasts—bleached oak blends with a stone countertop from Brač, another Croatian island.

Like a lookout set high up on the island, the tower is once again imposing and majestic. Landscape architect David Kelly, of RRP, designed and created the garden, populating it with trees like cypress, olive, and carob alongside the dry stone walls lining the plot.

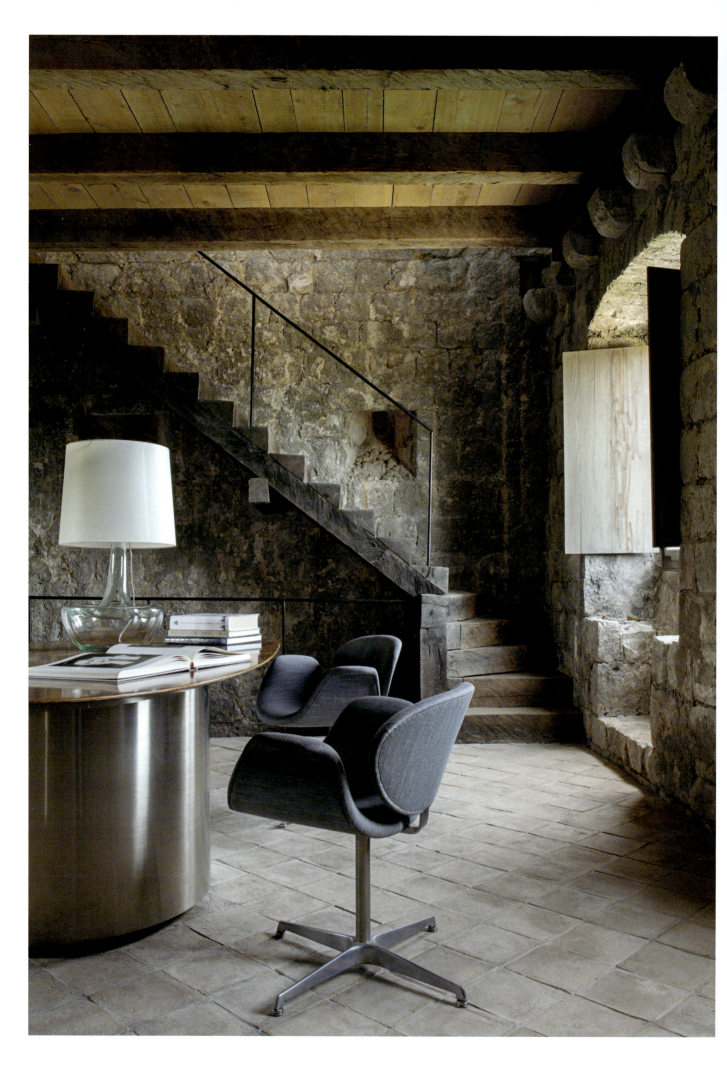

OPPOSITE
The reading room on the fourth level
takes up the whole floor. Lucien
Rees Roberts designed the oval
table especially for this space; it
was made in New York from a slab
of jacaranda taken from a house
by Oscar Niemeyer in Sao Paolo
and has a stainless steel base. Original Little Tulip chairs by Pierre
Paulin, 1965, issued by Artifort,
and the vintage glass lamp were
discovered in New York. Glass vase
from Paolo Venini. The floor is laid
with handmade terra-cotta tiles,
made in Italy by Fornace Stefani.

ABOVE
Inspired by a sixteenth-century
Venetian palace, the stairways in
Bosnian natural oak were made
to order and climb all the way to
the top floor. The metal rail was
made by a local craftsman.

PREVIOUS SPREAD
Steven Harris and Lucien Rees
Roberts created a huge living room
on the top floor of the tower. Its
built-in sofas are covered with
seats pads and cushions. A line of
ash-framed windows seems to invite
the astounding landscape in. This
spacious, understated reception
room has furnishings chosen from
among some of the great designer
names of the twentieth century.
Paillé original wood and straw
armchair by Charlottte Perriand,
c.1935; The Spanish Chair, 1950s oak
and leather chair by Danish designer
Børge Mogensen, Fredericia Furniture. Coffee tables designed by
Lucien, RRP; wood and leather
stools found in the United States.

RIGHT
For their bedroom, Steven and
Lucien decided on a mix of eras.
A 1965 artwork by Lucien's father,
Peter Rees Roberts, hangs on the
fifteenth-century stone wall. Murano
glass vases from the 1960s, the
armchair in original fabric and stainless steel footrest were bought in
the United States. The floor is laid
with terra-cotta tiles, from Fornace
Stefani. On the bed, washed linen
sheets, La Redoute Interiors.

OPPOSITE
The owners created a bespoke
glass-and-steel sliding window
so they could retain the original window opening. It is fixed
simply to the stone wall.

192

ARCHITECTURAL MINIMALISM

LE MARCHE, ITALY

PREVIOUS SPREAD
Casa Olivi enjoys a unique location nestled within a magnificent panoramic landscape; looking out past hills and villages as far as the Adriatic Sea.

OPPOSITE
The clean lines of the "365" outside furniture of Jose Gandia-Blasco for GANDIABLASCO are the perfect response to the rustic stones and the monumental proportions of this old farm turned vacation destination.

You can enjoy plenty of moments in the sun at this remarkable home built on the hills of Le Marche. In this unspoiled region of Italy, Swiss architects Markus Wespi and Jérôme de Meuron have transformed an old farm into a minimalist masterpiece that blends the traditional and the contemporary. With an approach that eschews excess, raw materials like stone, concrete, metal, and glass echo one another harmoniously.

Designated as a heritage site and partially destroyed by a fire, Casa Olivi has been given a new architectural aesthetic. "We wanted to keep the natural look of the old stones while infusing a striking modernity," explains Sophie, the owner. The structure retains its original character on the outside, while inside a series of white cubes create minimalist light-filled spaces. The hallway, kitchen/dining room, and living room ensemble is striking in its simplicity, opening into the stunning ancient landscape via large iron-framed glazed doors. The four bedrooms are arranged over two floors and have an almost monastic feel, completely devoid of excess.

The furniture for each space was designed by the architects and responds perfectly to the spirit of the location, avoiding any hint of distraction from the purity of architectural design. The clean lines and materials of the beds, tables, and desks chime perfectly with the exposed stone to balance rustic with sophisticated contemporary style. Outside, the estate has a hectare of olive and cypress trees and a sunken swimming pool surrounded by terra-cotta tiles—a blue ribbon that seems to hover between the sky and the land.

RIGHT
The contemporary-style kitchen is an exquisite blend of exposed stone, stainless steel, and a white resin floor. The central island from Arclinea features a discretely integrated hob, retractable hood, sink, and dishwasher extractor so as not to distract from the authenticity of the stone walls.

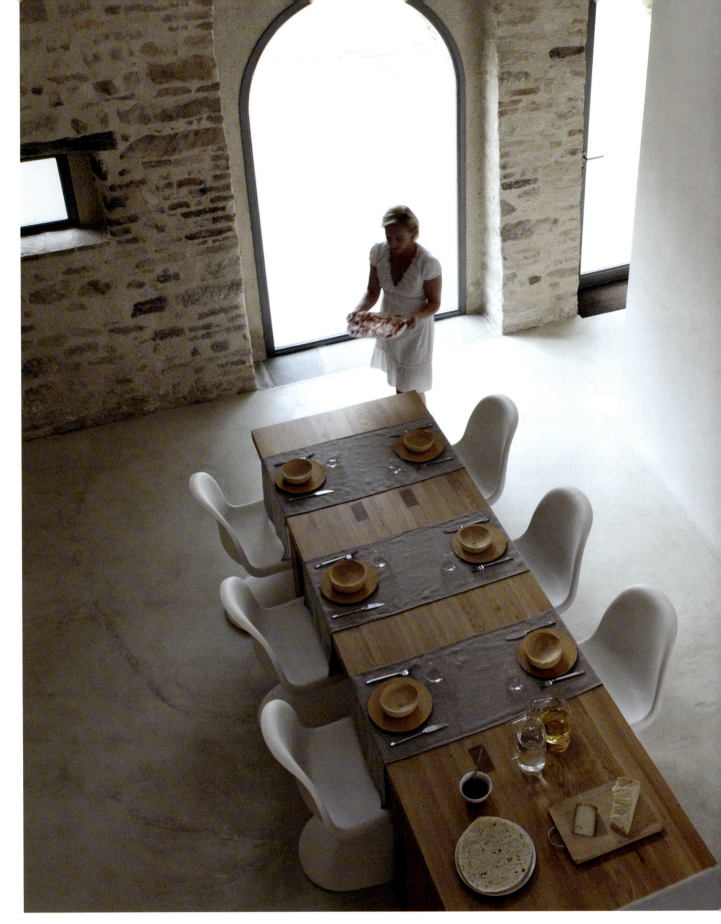

ABOVE
The dining room measures over
five meters in height and houses a
large bespoke table in natural oak
designed by Markus Wespi and
Jérôme de Meuron and made by the
2G joiners in Treia. The 1959 Panton
chairs by Verner Panton emphasize
the refined atmosphere of the room.

The swimming pool is located opposite the house on the east side;
the architects designed it so its
proportions work well with those
of the main building. The pool
and the stripped-back silhouette
of the "365" outside furniture by
Jose Gandia-Blasco for GANDIA-
BLASCO work perfectly together.

FOLLOWING SPREAD
A stone wall separates the two
living rooms whose Cassina
couches continue the clean-
lined style, along with a resin
floor and ironwork windows.
Wespi and de Meuron designed
the bespoke oak coffee tables.

ABOVE
Raw materials and bespoke furniture are made to work in harmony with the dimensions of the space—every detail has been considered, balancing simplicity with function.

ABOVE
The architects decided on a bold approach in the bedrooms: they designed and made the beds, the desks, and the en suite bathrooms. These different elements enhance the pared-back atmosphere. Washstand by Antonio Lupi, linen sheets by Caravane.

FOLLOWING SPREAD
Set in a wonderful natural environment, the façades and windows of the imposing farm retained their original form. Fully confident in their ability to balance the old with the new, Markus Wespi and Jérôme de Meuron designed a sleek twelve-by-five-meter aboveground swimming pool.

ABOVE
These slender, elegant porcelain
pieces are delicately edged in gold.

Anna Karin Andersson

UZÈS, FRANCE

"What I love most about my pieces are their imperfections. They give them something unique—a certain look, personality, and character." This is how Anna Karin Andersson, with her sparking blue eyes, bright smile, and long blond curls, describes her work. "I took part in a workshop with a ceramicist in my hometown of Gothenburg in Sweden when I was nine. I haven't stopped working with earth since then, dreaming up shapes to create into objects."

Her atelier is located in the center of the old town in Uzès. "I can work however I like here. I have space, natural light, and two powerful kilns. The perfect artist setup!" Her preferred material is porcelain that she works with whenever she can, using a variety of techniques—columbine, on a potter's wheel, or by pouring liquid porcelain into plaster molds she makes herself. Anna Karin uses a few different finishing techniques—textured, delicately colored in light tones, speckled, matte, and shiny—depending on her inspiration. Vases, cups, plates, side plates, carafes, bowls, candlestick holders—the artist sees her pieces as free spirits, leaving their flaws and imperfections untouched to occupy their own place. This approach characterizes her creations and lies at the very heart of her style. "I've always sought perfection, at school, then during higher education. But with ceramics, I feel free. I can see how beautiful flaws can be, and I've discovered a whole new universe where you can simply let go. I let the material speak for itself and come alive—this spontaneity gives my work a liberating, poetic authenticity." It's clear this ceramicist is both bold and boundlessly free.

Anna Karin Andersson in her studio with some of her smaller, unique pieces—in porcelain as always. Her extremely intuitive style highlights the imperfections that appear during the making process, unexpected elements that make each piece unique.

LEFT
"Liquid porcelain changed everything for me," says Anna Karin Andersson. "I discovered a new type of design. As a material, it brings me unbridled joy, and the clever use of plaster molds makes for a wonderful result!"

ABOVE
She has a particular affinity for working in white but sometimes decorates her pieces with blue or gold highlights, or with irregular speckles in deep blue.

OPPOSITE
Vase and bowl—porcelain crockery can take on hints of mint green or pale pink, like delicate flower petals.

PAST PERFECTED

DORDOGNE, FRANCE

PREVIOUS SPREAD
Two buildings nestle in the middle of a preserved natural setting, Le Four (the oven) and Le Moulin (the mill). Piet Hein Eek has completely renovated the ruins of this mill dating from the beginning of the nineteenth century: a splendid renovation, staggered over ten years.

OPPOSITE
Made with beams found on the site, the orange chest is a piece from the designer's collection. A collection of objects found here and there are arranged on top.

In the heart of the lush Périgord region of France, Dutch designer Piet Hein Eek's rural refuge is a little corner of paradise that blends subtly with its surroundings. This ancient mill nestles in a picturesque valley close to the hamlet of Mavaleix; restored using reclaimed materials, it is somewhere family and friends can now enjoy rustic retreats, surrounded by nature.

When Piet first discovered the dilapidated building, he was instantly bewitched; the ruin was ready to be rebuilt, and he felt deeply inspired. "My dream had always been to superimpose a contemporary style on an ancient foundation, to create a dialogue between past and present using what could be found in situ. It is the basis of all my work: to breathe new life into old materials," he explains. A forerunner of modern marquetry, Piet Hein Eek established himself as one of the pioneers of upcycling, notably with his Scrapwood technique, which consists of assembling wood offcuts. In a huge studio in Eindhoven, he and his team create furniture, lights, and unique items whose imperfections are testament to their rich history.

"I have never been attached to material possessions, but here, I felt the need to write a new chapter," he explains. He and his wife, Janine, committed to a lengthy project. "We wanted to understand the essence of the place. Because a mill is a little factory of yesteryear; everything worked in harmony with the natural elements—water, sun, stone, wood. That was the guiding light for this project." From the ruins, two separate buildings were born, each with a living room, kitchen, and three bedrooms, and a breathtaking view over the river. The majestic original frames were enhanced with furniture made from beams and pieces of wood found on-site. The works of designer and artist friends like Tom Dixon and Jan van de Ploeg, and Janine's tableware collection, enrich this world where boldness rubs shoulders with creativity.

RIGHT
The refreshing, lively river runs under the old mill, today transformed into a summer retreat for happy groups.

FOLLOWING PAGE
In Le Moulin, one of the two houses, a unique artwork by Dutch artist Jan van der Ploeg, covers an entire wall of the vast living room with colorful stripes. The sleek furniture comprises a sofa and a chair made by Piet Hein Eek from wood found among the ruins. The impressive chandelier by designer The Old Lampshade Lamp brings together a variety of vintage lampshades in frosted glass.

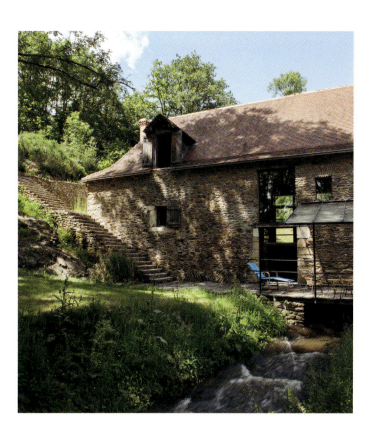

PREVIOUS PAGE
On the terrace of Le Four, Piet Hein Eek and his wife, Janine, have installed a lovely outside living room with furniture found in the region. A large bay window supported by beams found on the site bathes the inside living room with light.

ABOVE
In the kitchen of Le Moulin, the large table with rustic accents was made by Piet using recycled beams, painted in a blue shade that is used throughout both buildings. Glass lights by The Poor Silver Lampshade and bowl on base, Piet Hein Eek. Chairs found at a flea market.

OPPOSITE
Janine Hein Eeks' ultra-romantic, retro, blue-toned tableware collection was specially designed for the kitchen of Le Four. Today, it is sold in Piet Hein Eek's shop in Eindhoven in the Netherlands. The bespoke countertop and sideboard top in polished concrete sit between natural wood shelving and cupboard fronts.

OPPOSITE
A striking view over the river and
stunning surrounding nature from
one of the bedroom windows.

ABOVE
The walls are adorned with stripes
right to the top of the stairs to the
bedrooms, courtesy of Jan van de
Ploeg, a friend of the owner.

Beneath a majestic frame made
from reclaimed wood, this bedroom
brings together raw, rustic materials and contemporary lights. Lamp
with six silver balls, Tom Dixon,
and light installation created especially for the room by Piet Hein
Eek. The shelves were made by
the designer using pieces found at
a flea market. On the bed, yellow
linen sheets, La Redoute Interiors.

Leading from the primary bedroom,
the upper terrace offers breathtaking views over the Mediterranean Sea and a landscape of
olive groves and low stone walls—
so typical of the Balearics.

222

UNIQUE COLORS

MENORCA, SPAIN

PREVIOUS SPREAD
The architects from Atelier du Pont kept the original features of this old farm set in 36 hectares of virgin territory, while also introducing resolutely contemporary elements. Whitewashed facades, roofs covered in handmade tiles, gutters in the typical Menorcan style—all restored to an exceptional standard.

Menorca has long been a secret haven for a few French people in the know. Without her Spanish heritage, this little gem would likely have passed Maria by. "We were spellbound by the north of the island with its red earth and the sea that's turquoise one minute, green the next," she explains. For the couple and their five children, purchasing a 36-hectare plot was a revelation. "It was in the middle of nowhere, just how we'd always dreamed; at the end of a long lane edged by low stone walls. The *finca* was a ruin; a tornado had taken the roof and the surrounding greenery. There was a multitude of cramped, single-story buildings—the perfect bones for the best holidays in the world!"

Maria and her husband, Pierre, trusted Parisian architecture firm Atelier du Pont with the project. The firm was founded by Anne-Cécile Comar and Philippe Croisier; they knew how to mix vernacular artisanal traditions with subtle contemporary elements. Anne-Cécile Comar, who knows the island well, had carte blanche to do what she wanted with the 300-meter living space. "To give each room character, we envisaged solid colors in organic shapes to break up the rigidity of the spaces and disrupt the right angles of the very monochrome areas—to create quasi-dreamlike interior landscapes."

In the living room, your eyes are drawn to a majestic staircase with graceful curves, made using traditional Menorcan construction techniques to capture the light. The island is well-known for its talented artisans—you can see their golden touch in the joinery and furniture made by a local metalworker. Enthusiasm shines through every decision—in all the furniture discovered in Mahón, even in the Huguet Mallorca cement tiles decorating the kitchen—their apparently random placement belies a considered approach that becomes apparent once studied. This house is so much more than just a holiday home, it evokes a new version of the Mediterranean spirit.

RIGHT
Gently shaded from the sun, the summer seating area is an invitation to sit and relax. The owners found the bench, vintage rattan chairs, and coffee table in local antique stores.

OPPOSITE
Large organic shapes layered on
the living room walls introduce
energy and form into the large white
space of the house. Colors: Bone by
Farrow & Ball, and Sienne brûlée
by Argile. Two vintage chairs from
Can Sab Menorca sit on the wool
rug. The coffee tables are from
Bensimon. The pink metal stools are
by Indhia Mahdavi for Monoprix.

BELOW
The kitchen cupboards were custom
made for Atelier du Pont and painted
in Sienne brûlée by Argile. The
countertop and backsplash were
designed using Arta cement tiles
from the Alfredo Häberli collection, Huguet Mallorca. The original ventilation openings have been
kept and simply painted blue.

OPPOSITE
The four beds in the dormitory are
for the children. The architects opted
for shelving nooks in the wall to keep
the space clutter free. The sheets
and curved painted shape on the
wall both use a burnt earth palette.

ABOVE
The rooms are painted with unique
organic shapes in a variety of
earthy tones. The simple built-in
bed is covered by linen sheets
from La Redoute Interiors.

The wall of the two-tone shower
room is painted in Rouge du
Pozzuoli by Argile. Fuguet Demi-
Lune terrazzo tiles cover the floor.

FOLLOWING SPREAD
Adjacent to the living room, the
lounge is home to a magnificent
staircase leading to the second floor.
The vintage table and chairs were
found at Can Sab Menorca. The
cushions and seat pads on the iron
bench were custom-made in Yutes
linen. Set of embroidered cushions,
CFOC. Plain cushions, Maison de
Vacances. Two tapestries: the one on
the stairway by Tal Waldman, and in
the background by Picart Le Doux.

Atelier Vime

VALLABRÈGUES, FRANCE

OPPOSITE

Perched beneath the vaults of the eighteenth-century building, Atelier Vime's design studio is home to both contemporary creations and a selection of vintage furniture. Anthony Watson adds a variety of wicker shades to an Édith lamp in black metal. On the floor and ceiling, Gabriel pendant light in wicker and rattan. Front right, vintage rattan chair by French duo Audroux-Minet.

BELOW

Aramis ceiling light and Fifties floor lamp by Atelier Vime Éditions. The rattan couch is attributed to Louis Sognot. Tulip coffee table by Eero Saarinen (Knoll), Visage vase by DALO (50 cinquante) and drawings by Henri Ottmann.

On the top floor of the house, the attic is a wonderland in its own right with vintage piece upon vintage piece. Rattan table, chair, and lamp from the 1920s. On the wall, a collection of Vallauris ceramics from the nineteenth century.

On the banks of the Rhone, in the village of Vallabrègues, Hotel Drujon plays host to an experience from times gone by. This is where Benoît Rauzy and Anthony Watson launched Atelier Vime in 2016.

Vallabrègues was once surrounded by willows (whose young shoots provided wicker) and was home to almost four hundred and fifty basketmakers in the eighteenth and nineteenth centuries. "When we acquired Hotel Drujon, we took our role of preserving its heritage seriously," recalls Anthony. There are privately owned boutique hotels from the eighteenth century all over Provence, but this one was full of special details, such as the pools used to soften the wicker. It's as if continuing the basketmaking adventure, making it our own, was written in the place's history."

Atelier Vime's spirit lies in this willingness to build a bridge between the past and the present. Benoît and Anthony's contemporary creations have quickly charmed interior designers and architects like Pierre Yovanovitch, and the US market is also proving to be receptive. Karl Lagerfeld was an enthusiastic supporter from the beginning. The duo's tour de force is conquering the design world with subtle nods to retro style, new shapes that pay homage to times gone by. In addition to lights and their other creations, Atelier Vime offers select vintage pieces, chosen with the collecting duo's keen eye for design. Furniture by Gio Ponti, Jean Royère, Louis Sognot, Audoux-Minet, nineteenth-century ceramics from Vallauris, faience from Moustiers, terre mêlée from Uzès—their love of beauty and artisan work never runs dry.

ABOVE

The oversized Gabriel ceiling light in natural rattan comes in two models, 150 cm or 90 cm in diameter.

LEFT

Édith lamp, Atelier Vime Éditions, under an original print by Roger Capron. In the foreground, Soleil chair by Janine Abraham and Dirk Jan Rol, 1950s, painted emerald green.

The Médicis vase, a classic in natural rattan and wood, is made in two sizes, 18 cm and 27.5 cm tall. It is also available in a colored version. Here in its natural color, it stands out against the blue-gray wall (Berrington Blue by Farrow & Ball). Forged metal-and-wicker chair from the 1940s.

OPPOSITE

Installed beneath the rafters, a large bedroom with two 1950s rattan chairs by Gio Ponti and Lio Carminati, and a 1960s rattan table and a rattan cabinetry closet from the same era. Papier-mâché bull head by artist Claude Samson. Lamp with Cône shade, Atelier Vime Édition.

A LOVELY LOOKOUT

SKOPELOS, GREECE

PREVIOUS SPREAD
On the sloping terrain covered in
olive trees, Marc Held created an
octagonal central point, its dome
evoking an almost monastic feel.
Stone slates cover the roofs and the
walls are whitewashed, rendering
the buildings almost invisible and
in perfect harmony with the site.

OPPOSITE
This metal stairway is fixed simply
to the walls of the central structure and leads up to the roof. At
the top, the magnificent sweeping
view over the Aegean Sea and
the surrounding islands.

BELOW
In the main bedroom, the architect wanted to evoke a traditional Skopelos home, with an
exposed roof, a built-in bed, and
latticed wooden closet doors.

Near the clear waters of Skopelos, Parisian designer and architect Mark Held has successfully created a home that blends contemporary form with monastic gravity. It's as
though the gods of Mount Olympus were still shining down on this omnipotent nature,
bringing joy to the people. Greece's mythical legacy is more apparent here in the Spo-
rades islands than anywhere: in the beautiful turquoise sea, wild untouched coves, and
pine forests hugging the mountains.

The architect has lived here for over thirty years; he's famous for his remarkably
poetic and lyrical creations, and you can't help but admire the care he lavishes on finishing touches and bespoke designs. This summer home is no exception. Built diagonally
across a narrow, rocky plot, its two wings dock into a central section with a typically Mediterranean design of a large dome and neo-byzantine elements. Pared-back spaces evoke
a timeless aesthetic with exposed ceilings, terraces with jaw-dropping views, and paths
set with olive trees. The beauty of this location reigns supreme.

Despite being an artist whose creations embrace different eras and leapfrog playfully
from one decade to another, his work always acknowledges his beginnings. As a young
man, Marc Held found himself in Scandinavia where he had a front row seat to Arne
Jacobsen's design, Hans Webner's chairs and Poul Kjæholm's geometry. As a result, this
multitalented man focuses on creating dialogues between shapes and materials: wood,
stone, and metal. This timeless holiday home is a manifesto for an architecture that's
accessible to all.

PREVIOUS SPREAD
The main axis linking the two wings of the structure, the living room is a reinterpretation of Mediterranean style. Its large cupola allows cool air to flow naturally. In the center, looking out to sea, a large, U-shaped, polished concrete built-in sofa designed by the architect is covered with comfortable blue cotton cushions, Designers Guild, and green cushions, Caravane. In the background, Primo Culbuto fiberglass and leather chair, Marc Held.

ABOVE
Overlooking an untouched landscape, this outside living room makes for unforgettable holiday nights. Coffee tables, Habitat, built-in benches and cushions in washed linen.

OPPOSITE
The chic and elegant dining room combines a table designed by Mark Held and made to order by craftsman Nikos Ballas, and J39 chairs by the Danish designer Børge Mogensen, 1947, Fredericia Furniture. Colored glass vases, Habitat. Huge black metal lights with copper interiors hang from the ceiling, Davey Lighting. On the wall, a photo from the *Athos* series by Greek artist Stratos Kalafatis.

240

PREVIOUS SPREAD
Outside the main bedroom, the
private terrace hovers between the
sky and the sea. Simple choices and
pure lines; everything you need is
here. The daybed was a flea market
find, made-to-measure cotton cushions. Stools created from tree trunks.

OPPOSITE
Keeping vigil over the Aegean Sea
and surrounded by superb olive
groves tumbling down to the ocean.
The outside living room is blue and
white to blend into the environment.

BELOW
Below the house, this bedroom is
for friends passing through. It mixes
designer furniture with graphic
patterns. 1950s oak and leather
armchair The Spanish Chair by
Danish designer Børge Mogensen,
Fredericia Furniture; pure wool
flokati rug made in Greece. On the
wall, a photo from the *Archipelago*
series by artist Stratos Kalafatis.

A MESMERIZING RESURRECTION

UZÈS, FRANCE

PREVIOUS SPREAD
The outside living space melds into the charming, enclosed garden. In the foreground; a comfortable Bea Mombaers for Serax sofa, UDC store in Uzès, and Roly-Poly armchair by Faye Toogood for Driade. In the background, oak and straw chair, Midi Éditions. Metal coffee tables, Serax; amber-colored glasses, Ferm Living, and carafe, Fleux. Lights, natural fiber rug, and woolen cushions, Les Affaires Étrangères in Uzès.

OPPOSITE
Set in the middle of an interior courtyard, the swimming pool is surrounded by plants and shrubs from the region (grasses, pomegranate trees, and cypress, etc.) in a design by landscape architect Jean-Jacques Derboux, Les Jardins de la Calmette. Loungers and outside lights, Vincent Sheppard; ceramic stool, Serax, UDC.

Steel, concrete, and limewash—just some of the raw materials used in the brilliant redesign of a farm that had been left to slumber for decades. Today, the vast renovation project successfully melds a respect for its heritage with a sense of space, opening up rooms onto a private garden and a shaded pool. For Olivier and Stéphanie, the building is more than a house—it's a homecoming. After almost thirty years of living in England, and raising two children in London, the couple dreamed of the wild brush, of vines and the sun. This rare gem of a building was hiding in a small village in the Gard region of southern France. An old farm connected to a chateau; weathered by time but full of history.

"We wanted to breathe life back into this magnificent building," Olivier recollects. The challenge was to retain its soul and to reinvent the space without meddling with the building's essence. Original architectural elements like the monumental timber roofs, the terra-cotta *parefeuille* tiles decorating the ceilings and roofs, and the majestic ashlar vaults had to be conserved, but more important, be placed at the core of the project. The living room is the heart of the house in what were once the stables. It opens onto a covered terrace, offering continual dialogue between the indoors and the outdoors.

Olivier is passionate about architecture while Stéphanie loves interior design; they had a specific vision for the renovation. They called on Nîmes architect Anthony Pascual and his network of craftsmen to turn their vision a reality. Stéphanie opted for a combination of contemporary and antique pieces for the interior. "We also designed bespoke elements with Anthony, particularly the magnificent raw steel stairway which is a focal point of the renovation," Olivier acknowledges gratefully.

A timeless resurrection. It's as though the farm's transformation is simply a continuation of its story. As the writer William Faulkner said, "The past is never dead. It's not even past."

RIGHT
Stéphanie chose all the furniture, pottery, and lights to ensure harmony with the building. An artwork by artist Balthazar Beauzon and pottery found locally sit on a vintage chest of drawers from Les Affaires Étrangères.

RIGHT
The owners created a lovely dining room in one wing of the house to enjoy summer meals in the shade. The long wooden table was discovered on Steph Since 1979, an online marketplace; benches from Moustique in Arles. Terracotta lights, La Maison Pernoise.

PREVIOUS SPREAD
The vaulted ceiling of the old stables; this huge room now houses the kitchen made from stained oak veneer by a local carpenter with a countertop in blue Portuguese stone. Cadieras oak-and-straw chairs from Midi Éditions line the bespoke steel table designed by Thomas Cortes, Métallerie Cortes in Nîmes. Lights, Les affaires étrangères in Uzès.

OPPOSITE
In the living room adjacent to the kitchen, stone and earth accents mix with those of the linen sofas, Maison de Vacances, the armchairs, Midi Éditions, the natural fiber lights, Les affaires étrangères, and the coffee table made from an old barn door found on-site.

ABOVE
You access the other floors from the hallway via a superb bespoke steel stairway made by the metal-worker Thomas Cortes. The polished concrete floor is an elegant response to the rough shuttered concrete ceiling. The tapestry *Les Touches de sable* (2023) by Julie Robert is displayed on the wall. Wooden bench, Atmosphère d'ailleurs.

ABOVE
In the upstairs office, a Maison de
Vacances sofa topped by Casa-
mance cushions, a Roly-Poly by Faye
Toogood armchair for Driade, and a
rattan lamp by Ferm Living create a
cozy living area. A piece by English
artist Robert Stewart is displayed
on the wall, from 50 cinquante
gallery in L'Isle-sur-la-Sorgue.

OPPOSITE
Beneath the bedroom's rafters,
Stéphanie opted for rattan lights
from Faro Barcelona that work
perfectly with the Maison de
Vacances headboard, and with
the linen sheets in the colors
of Provence by Merci. Rug, Les
affaires étrangères in Uzès. On
the left, an untitled work by
artist Caroline Beauzon.

254

ABOVE
In the primary bedroom, the metal headboard forms a kind of cocoon. A large closet by carpenter Bernard Florenchie, Sur Mesure Concept in Nîmes cleverly separates the bathroom area. The bed is made up with hemp sheets, Couleur Chanvre, linen throw and cushions, Maison de Vacances. Bedside table, Polspotten; lights, Ay Illuminate.

Beneath the pitched roof, featuring a superb checkers pattern created with *parefeuilles* tiles found on-site, this gray room brings together a bed made up with anthracite-colored linen, a blanket from UDC in Uzès, linen sheets, Merci, and bedspread, Cultiver. The lime-wash on the walls is a shade created by Demba Coulibaly, ETR Façades in Nîmes. Wicker bull head found at L'Isle-sur-la-Sorgue.

OPPOSITE
Olivier and Stéphanie wanted a double shower with a concrete floor, walls covered in Zellig tiles and *tadelakt* by artisan Demba Coulibaly. Taps and fittings, Officina Nicolazzi. Stool, Atmosphère d'ailleurs, towel and bath mat, Ferm Living.

OPPOSITE

The green-and-cream color scheme of the Backgammon kitchen tiles is reflected in the Hex Crossroads floor tiles. Staff can eat their lunch at the bar. The rattan lights were found in souks.

Popham Design
MARRAKECH, MOROCCO

Caitlin and Samuel Dowe-Sandes are the exuberant founders of Popham Design in Marrakech. Their ultra-graphic cement tiles bring traditional Moroccan artisan craft into the twenty-first century, with an endless variety of collections and designs. The infinitely creative New York couple have lived in Morocco for almost two decades, although they travel almost constantly around the globe. They discovered their passion almost by chance in 2007 when they were renovating their medina riad and they decided to design tile for use in the restoration themselves. Success quickly followed, with their designs crossing borders to adorn restaurants, hotels, luxury houses, and city apartments. The couple have continued to create in their studio and workshop close to Marrakech ever since that first moment of inspiration, producing patterned collections in subtle tones, an endless array of different shades, and shimmering Zellige tile collections.

Carefully made by hand using local materials like cement and marble dust, Popham tiles are free from lead and toxins, making them both durable and environmentally friendly. The use of a hydraulic press rather than a kiln, like ceramic tiles, means very little energy goes into their production; the process also includes systems for reclaiming water at every stage.

The factory has a staff of sixty with Caitlin and Samuel's showroom and design studio just a stone's throw away. Unique graphic tiles in different shades of green—a symbol of hope—cover every part of the lounge, kitchen, and office. The location itself serves as stimulation for ideas for new designs and color ranges: also inspiring architects, decorators, and clients on a quest for their perfect pattern—an almost impossible choice.

ABOVE & RIGHT

A corner for relaxing in the office. Arch tiles on the floor feature a 1960s-inspired wave pattern. Biscuit, Emerald, Envy, Oyster, Milk . . . the huge variety of Popham tiles includes 140 shades and over a hundred original designs by Samuel and Caitlin Dowe-Sandes.

ABOVE

The couple with their daughter next to their old Renault 4L.

OPPOSITE
Samuel and Caitlin Dowe-Sandes
mixed shapes and colors in their riad,
even going as far as decorating the
bedrooms with cement tiles in subtle
color combinations—here the wall is
adorned with Tate cement tiles. The
floor and walls of the bathroom in
the background have been laid with
Hex Artichoke tile in Slate/Indigo.

ABOVE
Popham Design has been making
Zellige tiles for several years;
they come in a superb range of
colors. Each cement tile is made
by hand in the workshop.

SEVENTIES VIBES

UZÈS, FRANCE

PREVIOUS SPREAD
On the top floor of the monumental building, Eva Gnaedinger furnished the spacious living room with pieces from the 1970s, patiently discovered throughout Europe over time. She loves the contrast between the old stone and the design elements.

OPPOSITE
Olive trees in the courtyard of the old presbytery. Here Eva installed a 3.6 × 2.4 m pool edged with large stones. A pleasantly cool corner in the summer.

You need to follow your instinct when you're choosing a house. So says interior designer Eva Gnaedinger, who regularly renovates beautiful buildings in the Uzès region of France, bringing them back to life. Eva, who is of Swiss origin and an avid globetrotter, has a knack for finding hidden gems—even when they're covered with linoleum, fitted carpets, plaster, or gaudy tiles. This time, a 1936 presbytery caught her eye; she has a particular affinity for dry stone, whitewash, and soft colors.

Luckily, local artisans had the skills to help her with the project. It took four long years to take the building from darkness to light: by opening up spaces, knocking down walls, and stripping down beams to realize Eva's vision. She knew this construction site was destined to become somewhere beautiful. She installed a pool, riad style, in the interior courtyard and created interplay between the rooms of the four-story house through colors and textures. Several rooms have blue, cream, gray-beige tones or vintage-patterned wallpaper, with their own bathroom, and selected stone walls are exposed for a sense of timeless charm. Eva was meticulous in her choice of colors, her decisions becoming clearer when she thought about each room as part of the ensemble. She created balance by considering the relationship between architectural details, furnishings, and the wonderful lights she found in the markets of Italy, France, Switzerland, and Los Angeles, her home for a decade or so. The objects she chose also contribute to the ambience; they are the fruit of much searching and show off her love of the 1970s with an eclectic mix of materials and accents from 1960–70 in beautifully considered combinations.

RIGHT
The charming kitchen doubles as a dining room. It has an old table and chairs from the 1960s discovered at garage sales. The ceiling light and the artwork are from a Villeneuve-lès-Avignon flea market.

A masterpiece: the stone stairway links the three floors of the building.

Laurent Mura, a local stonemason, created a superb fireplace in Bourgogne stone beneath the vaults of Eva's atelier, with limewashed walls. A pair of lamps sit on the fireplace with a 1970s petal light on the wall, found in Ticino, Switzerland. Murano vases bought in Italy. Pistillo ceiling light by Studio Tetrarch, Valenti Luce edition from the 1960s.

The superb stairway dates from when the presbytery was built in 1868. Rattan chairs from an Uzès flea market. Blue Vallauris pottery fountain from 1960, found at the Déballage trade market in Avignon.

266

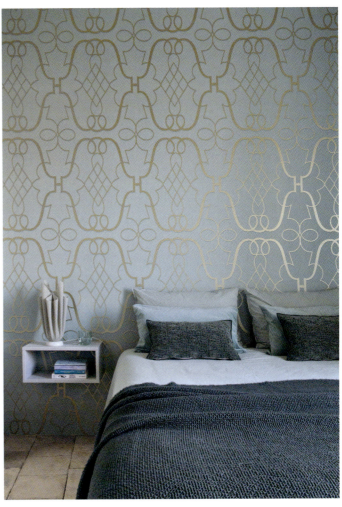

OPPOSITE

In the first-floor living room Eva Gnaedinger chose Farrow & Ball Railing black paint for a whole wall, with the others in Cornforth White. Sofa, IKEA; cushions, Maison de Vacances and throw, Society Limonta. Coffee table, golden stool, raindrop chandelier, lamp, and Murano glass wall light from Avignon, Switzerland, and Italy. An artwork by Berlin artist Kiddy Citny hangs on the wall. On the fireplace, which has been preserved in its original state, vases from regional markets.

ABOVE

Every bedroom has its own color. Here, pale blue is the predominant color; it is seen in the wallpaper, wall paint, linen sheets, and woolen throw. The armchair and vase are vintage finds.

ABOVE

Eva Gnaedinger created a huge dining room on the top floor combining rugs from Morocco's High Atlas and Les affaires étrangères in Uzès, a vintage table from Los Angeles, metal chairs bought from a local secondhand store, and Panton chairs by Verner Panton, 1959. The glass 1960s ceiling light is from Emmaüs in Ticino, Switzerland.

OPPOSITE

In her cathedral-like bedroom that measures over seven meters in height, Eva left the walls in dry stone and lime render. The bed has linen sheets and a wool throw, Society Limonta. The bedside light is from Los Angeles, and Eva made the lampshade. In the three niches, *Le Baise*, a sculpture by stonemason Laurent Mura, a pink flamingo found at a Villeneuve-lès-Avignon flea market, and a molding found in Los Angeles.

"HAPPY THE MAN WHO, LIKE ULYSSES…"

MYKONOS, GREECE

PREVIOUS SPREAD

The enormous terrace enjoys spectacular views over the Aegean Sea and the island of Tinos from the shade of a pergola of sweet chestnut and eucalyptus branches. The outside living room is furnished with three Edge sofas, teak stools and coffee tables from Samba, Anton, and Rex from Gommaire. Indigo Santa Fe and Havana Lido cushions, Maison de Vacances.

OPPOSITE

The entire length of the large sitting room opens onto a terrace with Mediterranean views, a striking olive tree at its center, and two Lana Deco papier-mâché urns. Low stool by Pierre Frey in Alexander fabric, Gervasoni sofa with linen cushions from Maison de Vacances. Moroccan pottery vases and candlestick holders from Les affaires étrangères in Uzès.

RIGHT

The raw stone central island in the outdoor kitchen also serves as a bar and somewhere to enjoy a quick salad with delicious fresh fish.

PAGE 276

Nikos Adrianopoulos designed the kitchen. The huge four-meter teak table adjoining the lava stone island was imagined for the space by Lola Séguéla. Benches and teak stools by Gommaire. Striped ceramics, plates from Sejnane. Tamegroute bowls, jug and salad bowls; Doum palm (palm fiber) lights, Les affaires étrangères. The natural oak ceiling was painted white.

PAGE 277

The stunning décor of the outside dining room. A pergola of sweet chestnut and eucalyptus branches casts welcome shade over a bespoke solid teak table and Sally chairs from Gommaire. Cast concrete Luna lights, Urbi et Orbi.

The Cyclades—including Naxos, Sifnos, Paros—are places to dream of all year long. Then summer arrives and there they are with the sea stretching out ahead, a bursting blue sky, and epic sunsets. And then there's Mykonos. You might think it would be crowded, but here you'll find only calm. The house is set on a bare coastal landscape, opposite the island of Syros. "It's such a magical and inspiring place," exclaims interior designer Lola Séguéla of Studio Séguéla. "When I discovered Nikos Adrianopoulos's unique architecture and understood its beauty, I knew I had to create a design full of integrity, one that wouldn't try to compete with it. I've always tried to use materials and colors in my work that are in harmony with the landscape. And that was absolutely the right approach here."

The owners also prefer understated style; their wish was for a contemporary look with neutral colors that highlighted the exceptional sweeping views over the sea and the wild rocky island. "The owners played a big part in the project," adds Lola. "Together we checked every detail. I ordered furniture for a whole year and stored it in a warehouse. I had more than twenty different suppliers! In the end it felt like I'd solved a huge puzzle."

The west-facing Cycladic haven covers over a thousand square meters, with terraces, communal spaces, intimate suites, and a house reserved for guests. Architect Nikos Adrianopoulos circles back to the original aim of the project: "I wanted to create something authentic that responded to the natural light. I imagined wells of light and openings that infused life into the all the living spaces." The Greeks have been finding the balance between majesty and aesthetic rigor since ancient times.

PREVIOUS SPREAD
An outside living room close to the
swimming pool is a lovely lookout
point. Lola Séguéla designed a long
built-in bench with bespoke seats
and cushions made in outdoor
fabric from Gommaire and natural
fabric from Les affaires étrangères
in Uzès. Teak table, Gommaire;
braided rope stools, Sempre; rope
light, Les affaires étrangères. The
round natural fiber mat on the
wall is from Tozeur in Tunisia.

OPPOSITE
In one of the house's seven
bedrooms a wall is covered with
polished oak planks that have
been stained gray. Palm fiber light.
Braided abaca fiber mat on the wall,
Brucs. On the bed, hemp linens,
Couleur Chanvre; honeycomb fabric
throw, Haomy; embroidered linen
cushion, Evolution Product. Bedside
table in smoked teak, Gommaire.

ABOVE
Each bedroom has a seating area
in brown and ochre tones. Ethni-
craft cushions arranged on a
Studio Séguéla linen sofa. Terra-
cotta lamp from Gafsa, Les affaires
étrangères. Eichholtz rug with three
wooden stools from Polspotten.
Abstract artworks, FormWorks.

The sleek, refined bathrooms feature
a combination of wood and resin.

ABOVE
The idyllic view over neighboring islands from the 26 × 4 m swimming pool; the comfy Gommaire daybeds set along the length of the pool are an invitation to laze.

OPPOSITE
The house is west-facing and set partly into the rockface, with large terraces cut into the slope. In front of each bedroom, simple built-in benches are shaded by wooden pergolas. You can make the most of the spectacular natural surroundings from these intimate spaces. Occasional tables, Gommaire.

Majestic Peace (pp. 6-17)
Architect: Antonio Zaninovic
www.antoniozaninovic.com
Architecture: Steven Harris Architects
www.stevenharrisarchitects.com
@stevenharrisarchitects
Interior Design: RRP
(formerly Rees Roberts + Partners)
www.reesroberts.com
@reesrobertspartners

Mountains and Marvels (pp. 18-27)
Architects: Oro Del Negro and Manuel
Villanueva, Moredesign
www.moredesign.es

A Haven on High (pp. 28-39)
Architecture and Interior Design:
Atelier du Pont, architects
Associates: Anne-Cécile Comar and Philippe Croisier
9, impasse Lamier F-75011 Paris
Tel.: + 33 1 53 33 24 10
www.atelierdupont.fr
@atelierdupont
The house is available for rent: www.esbecdaguila.com
@esbecdaguila

Adriana Meunié and Jaume Roig (pp. 40-45)
https://adrianameunie.wordpress.com/
@adrianameunie_textilework
https://jaumeroigceramica.wordpress.com/
@jaumeroig_artwork

Art at Its Heart (pp. 46-57)
Mas Re.Source
1328, chemin du Terme F-30630 Montclus
www.masresource.fr
@mas_resource
Architect: Lucilla de Montis, agency
DirectArchitecte
www.directarchitecte.fr
Rémy and Marc Étienne-Coussedière
Tel.: + 33 6 73 23 26 73
contact@masresource.fr

A Rural Aesthetic (pp. 58-69)
Son Blanc Farmhouse
www.sonblancmenorca.com
@sonblancmenorca
Architecture and Interior Design:
Atelier du Pont Agency, Architects
Associates: Anne-Cécile Comar and
Philippe Croisier Agency
9, impasse Lamier F-75011 Paris
Tel. : + 33 1 53 33 24 10
www.atelierdupont.fr
@atelierdupont

La Scourtinerie (pp. 70-73)
https://www.scourtinerie.com/
@lascourtinerie

The Perfect Place to Perch (pp. 74-85)
Architect: Thomas Fourtané,
Archipetrus agency in Porto-Vecchio
www.archipetrus.com
@archipetrus
Interior Designer: Claire Euvrard,
Numero 15 agency in Paris
www.numero15.fr
@claire_euvrard

A Sunny Retreat (pp. 86-97)
Architects: Sotiris Tsergas and Katja
Margaritoglou, Block 722 agency
14 Ardittou Street GR-Athènes 11636
Tel.: + 30 210 3617081
Stureplan 4C S-Stockholm 114 35
Such.: + 46 70 4526505
www.block722.com
@block722architects

Paola Paronetto (pp. 98-101)
https://www.paolaparonetto.com
@paolaparonettocreations

The House of Straw and Azure Blue (pp. 102-111)
Architect: Nuno Lopes
@nuno_lopes_architecture
Barracuda Interiors Gallery in Lisbon
www.barracuda-interiors.com
@barracuda_interiors

Summer on the Slopes (pp. 112-123)
Architect: Rudy Flament
www.ahaarchitecture.com/rudy-flament
Interior Designer: Marie-Laure Helmkampf
@mlhelmkampf

Laurent Passe (p. 124-129)
https://www.laurentpasse.com/
@laurentpasse

Open Spaces (p. 130-139)
Masseria Le Carrube
www.masserialecarrubeostuni.it/en

Delicate Materials (p. 140-149)
Mascal
The house can be rented: @mascal_uzes

Jean-Luc Mare (p. 150-153)
http://www.jeanlucmare.com/
@jeanlucmareluminaires

Augmented Radicality (p. 154-167)
Architect: Gonçalo Bonniz
www.gbarquitectos.pt
Decorators: Emma Pucci and Valentina Pilia,
Flores Textiles Studio
www.florestextilestudio.com
@flores_textilestudio

A Special View (p. 168-179)
Architects: Clarisse Labro and Mark Davis,
Labro & Davis agency
www.labrodavis.com
@labrodavis

Ghislaine Garcin (pp. 180-183)
https://www.ghislainegarcin.fr/
@ghislainegarcin

Tour of the Tower (pp. 184-193)
Architecture: Steven Harris Architects
www.stevenharrisarchitects.com
@stevenharrisarchitects
Interior Design: RRP agency
(formerly Rees Roberts + Partners)
www.reesroberts.com
@reesrobertspartners

Architectural Minimalism (pp. 194-205)
Architects: Markus Wespi
and Jérôme de Meuron,
Wespi de Meuron Romeo agency
www.wdmra.ch
@wespidemeuronromeo

Anna Karin Andersson (p. 206-209)
Anna Karin Ceramics
9, rue Port-Royal F-30700 Uzès
www.annakarinceramique.com
@annakarin.ceramique

Past Perfected (pp. 210-219)
Piet Hein Eek
www.pietheineek.nl
@piet_hein_eek
The two houses, the Oven and the Mill, are
available for rent: pietheineek.nl/en/news/
holidays-in-mavaleix
info@pietheineek.nl

Unique Colors (pp. 220-229)
Architecture and Interior Design:
Atelier du Pont agency, architects
associates: Anne-Cécile Comar and
Philippe Croisier agency
9, impasse Lamier F-75011 Paris
Tel. : + 33 1 53 33 24 10
www.atelierdupont.fr
@atelierdupont

Atelier Vime (pp. 230-233)
https://ateliervime.com/
@ateliervime

A Lovely Lookout (pp. 234-245)
Architect-designer: Marc Held
www.marcheldarchitect.com/fr

A Mesmerizing Resurrection (pp. 246-257)
Architect: Anthony Pascual,
Pascual Architecte agency
www.pascualarchitecte.fr
@pascual_architecte

Popham Design (pp. 258-261)
7 km Ourika Road
Tassoultante, Marrakech
www.pophamdesign.com
contact@pophamdesign.com
@pophamdesign
Showroom:
60, rue du Vertbois F-75003 Paris
paris@pophamdesign.com

Seventies Vibes (pp. 262-271)
Eva Gnaedinger
@evagnaedinger

"Happy the man who, like Ulysses…" (pp. 272-283)
Architect: Nikos Adrianopoulos,
Architecture & Lighting Design
www.nikosadrianopoulos.com
@nikos_adrianopoulos
Designer: Lola Séguéla, Studio Séguéla
www.studioseguela.com
@studioseguela

Laurence Dougier, a journalist and stylist specializing in interior design, collaborates with several French interior magazines (*Elle Décoration*, *Côté Sud*, *Marie-Claire Maison*, *Madame Figaro*, etc.) and various international magazines (*House & Garden*, *Elle Decor*, *Veranda*, etc.). She is the author, with Frédéric Couderc and photographer Deidi von Schaewen, of the book *Inside Africa* (Taschen).

Nicolas Mathéus regularly works with major international interior design magazines such as *Elle Décoration*, *Côté Sud*, *Marie-Claire Maison*, etc. He is the author, with Catherine Scotto for the texts, of *Maroc. Art de vivre et création* (Éditions de La Martinière, 2022).

ACKNOWLEDGMENTS

This book is the culmination of years of collaboration with various magazines.

Laurence Dougier and Nicolas Mathéus warmly thank Sylvie de Chirée and Catherine Scotto, Danièle Gerkens and Clémence Leboulanger (*Elle Décoration*), Françoise Lefébure and Martine Duteil (*Côté Sud*), Anne Desnos and Sylvie Éloy (*Marie Claire Maison*), Emmanuelle Eymery and Vanessa Zocchetti (*Madame Figaro*), and all their wonderful teams. Your support and loyalty made all this possible.

We also thank the owners, architects, interior designers, and decorators for their trust.

Nicolas Mathéus thanks Bettina Lafond for the report on La Scourtinerie in Nyons.

MEDITERRANEAN LIVING
Originally published in French as *Plein Sud*
by Éditions de La Martinière, Paris
First published in English in 2025 by The Vendome Press
Vendome is a registered trademark of The Vendome Press LLC

VENDOME PRESS US
PO Box 566
Palm Beach, FL 33480

VENDOME PRESS UK
Worlds End Studio
132–134 Lots Road
London, SW10 0RJ

www.vendomepress.com

Copyright © 2025 Éditions de La Martinière, a trademark
of EDLM, 57 rue Gaston Tessier, 75019 Paris
English translation copyright © 2025 The Vendome Press LLC

All rights reserved. No part of the contents of this
book may be reproduced in whole or in part without
prior written permission from the publisher.

Any use of this book to train generative artificial intelligence
("AI") technologies is expressly prohibited.
Vendome Press, their authors, and their photographers reserve
all rights to license uses of this work for generative AI training
and development of machine learning language models.

ISBN 978-0-86565-475-4

Publishers Beatrice Vincenzini, Mark
Magowan, and Francesco Venturi

Translators Rhiannon Egerton & Debbie Garrick
Production Director Jim Spivey
Designer Mark Melnick

Library of Congress Cataloging-in-Publication
Data available upon request.

Distributed in North America by:
Abrams Books
www.abramsbooks.com

Distributed in the Rest of the World by:
Thames & Hudson Ltd.
6-24 Britannia Street
London WC1X 9JD
United Kingdom
www.thamesandhudson.com

EU Authorised Representative:
Interart S.A.R.L.
19 rue Charles Auray
93500 Pantin, Paris
France
productsafety@vendompress.com
www.interart.fr

Printed and bound in Slovenia

First Printing

PHOTO CREDITS AND COPYRIGHTS
[T: top, b: bottom, l: left, r: right, m: middle]
All photographs are by Nicolas Mathéus except:
pp. 40, 42bl, 44, and 45: Adriana Meunié; p. 41l: Ricard
Lopez for Plus Magazine; p. 41r: Ritchie Jo; p. 42tl: Barbara
Vidal for Pedro Garcia; pp. 98 to 101: Studio Auber.

OTHER COPYRIGHTS
Despite our extensive research, and due to sometimes incomplete
information, it was not possible to identify certain works, and the
copyright holders for certain documents could not be located. For
this purpose, an account has been opened in our accounts for them.

© Adagp, Paris, 2025: pp. 9, 13, 191: Paillé armchair by Charlotte
Perriand; p. 10l: pendant lamp by Isamu Noguchi; p. 11: painting
by John Murray; p. 115l: Oase armchair by Wim Rietveld; p. 147,
197, 198, 202r: Panton chairs by Verner Panton; p. 180, 181, 182, 183:
works by Ghislaine Garcin; p. 188: Little Tulip armchairs by Pierre
Paulin; pp. 212–219: creations by Piet Hein Heek; pp. 228–229 (in
the background): tapestry by Jean Picart Le Doux; p. 233bl: print
by Roger Capron; p. 12: desk by Bodil Kjær and painting by Ursula
McCannell; pp. 14–15: side tables by Eero Saarinen, Courtesy
of Knoll, Inc.; p. 30: painting *Eagle's Break* by Ezra Siegel; p. 38:
painting *Composition* by Paloma Peláez Bravo; p. 51: photographs
of *La Photocopieuse* by Julien Benard; p. 54: photographs from the
"Windows" series by Luc Dratwa; p. 55: Resinotype by Gérard
Traquandi; p. 56: Photographs of *Humanity Man 1:27 a.m.* and
Humanity Women 2:22 a.m. by Lucie de Barbuat and Simon Brodbek;
p. 82-83: C317 armchairs by Yuzuru Yamakawa for Feelgood Designs;
p. 95: Chairs by Hans Wegner and Carl Hansen; p. 106: Forests
of Trees tapestry by Anne Laure and table by Paul Frankl; p. 107:
Fresco by Redfield & Dattner, chairs by Colette Gueden, and 1725
armchairs by Warren Platner, Courtesy of Knoll, Inc.; p. 111d: *Trees
in the City* tapestry by Anne Laure; p. 117: section by Pascale Saint-
Sorny; p. 142: painting by Martial Michaux; p. 162-163: *Landscape
Site 3* painting by Nicolas Lefeuvre for the gallery Jean-François-
Cazeau; p. 176: table by Pierre Chapo and Golden Bell pendants
by Alvar Aalto for Artek; p. 178-179: low chairs by Raoul Guys; p.
186: Tulip chairs by Eero Saarinen, Courtesy of Knoll, Inc.; p. 191,
245: armchair The Spanish Chair by Børge Mogensen for Fredericia
Furniture; p. 196, 199: furniture from the "365" collection by Jose
Gandia-Blasco for GANDIABLASCO; p. 214, 219g: wall by Jan van
der Ploeg; p. 228-229 (in the staircase): tapestry by Tal Waldman –
Talva D.; p. 231g: Tulip table by Eero Saarinen, Courtesy of Knoll,
Inc.; p. 241: photograph from the "Athos" series by Stratos Kalafatis
and J39 chairs by Børge Mogensen for Fredericia Furniture; p. 245:
photograph from the "Archipelago" series by Stratos Kalafatis; pp.
246-247, 254: Roly Poly armchair by Faye Toogood for Driade; p.
249l: painting by Balthazar Beauzon; p. 253: tapestry "Les Touches de
sable" by Julie Robert; p. 254: painting by © Robert Stewart/Centre
For Advanced Textiles, The Glasgow School of Art; p. 255: painting
by Caroline Beauzon; p. 266: fireplace by Laurent Mura; p. 268:
painting by Kiddy City; p. 271: sculpture "The Kiss" by Laurent Mura.